ENDORS

Inked for Eternity took my faith to a new level! It is an inspiring story of strength, healing, and perseverance. I couldn't put it down. I can honestly say this book has helped me to embrace and live the life God has planned for me.

ASHLEE TALASKI

Roxanne takes us on a journey of heartache, depression, and renewal ending in a miracle of love and faith restored. I am honored to be a part of her story.

STEPHEN ROBERTS

This book will totally transform and inspire anyone who reads it. This is a must read for everyone from all walks of life.

DR. JAMES AND JOY NASH
First Church of the Nazarene
Fort Walton Beach, Florida

I became a prisoner of hope, captivated by this book. It was full of hope, healing, and heaven. Writings like this help put perspective to a myopically challenged generation. It's one of those books I want to read over and over to keep my focus as it should be—heaven bound.

REBECCA KELLEY

Inked for Eternity meant a lot to me. I am 15 years old and was going through some tough things before I read this book. I questioned everything about myself, especially my faith. Roxanne's story helped me figure out who I am, and it answered so many questions about God and heaven. After reading this, I have become confident in who I am as a Christian and a person.

LYDIA GIVENS

I would highly recommend this book. It reminded me of God's faithfulness in all areas of my life physically, emotionally, and spiritually. When things look their bleakest and we're ready to give up, God is there, waiting patiently to pick up the shattered pieces to create something beautiful in the midst of the pain. He only asks that we trust Him.

DEBRA PAHL

INKED *for* ETERNITY

INKED *for* ETERNITY

LIVING IN THE LIGHT OF HEAVEN ON EARTH

ROXANNE WERMUTH WITH PETER LUNDELL

DESTINY IMAGE® PUBLISHERS, INC.

P.O. Box 310, Shippensburg, PA 17257-0310

"Promoting Inspired Lives."

This book and all other Destiny Image and Destiny Image Fiction books are available at Christian bookstores and distributors worldwide.

Cover design by: Christian Rafetto

Published in association with the literary agency of
Credo Communications, LLC, Grand Rapids, Michigan,
www.credocommunications.net.

For more information on foreign distributors, call 717-532-3040.
Reach us on the Internet: www.destinyimage.com.

ISBN 13 TP: 978-0-7684-0741-9
ISBN 13 eBook: 978-0-7684-0742-6

For Worldwide Distribution, Printed in the U.S.A.
1 2 3 4 5 6 7 8 / 19 18 17 16 15

DEDICATION

To the memory of my father and the tumultuous journey our lives traveled to a final destination of love and reconciliation.

ACKNOWLEDGMENTS

I am thankful to so many people:

- The staff at Destiny Image, for having faith in me.

- Daniel V. Wermuth, for cover portraits.

- Rev. David E. Wermuth, you are the very first person I had the courage to share my experience with. You listened and encouraged me to write my story. Thank you, Dad.

- Rev. James Franklin, for insisting I write my story.

- My entire family, for your ongoing support and encouragement.

- Karen Neumair, our agent at Credo Communications who worked long hours on this project.

- Gayle Anderson, my new friend in Minnesota who helped us so much by reading and critiquing the manuscript.

- Muriel Lundell, for insisting that your son write this book.

- Peter Lundell, for writing my story so beautifully. It is nearly impossible for me to express my gratitude for what Peter has done. He worked patiently with me, getting to know me so well as to write my life's story in *my* voice with *his* words. I am truly amazed with his talent and the effort he made. Thank you, Peter.

- David, my devoted husband. Thank you for loving me unconditionally, taking me for better or worse, in sickness and health and supporting me all the way through this journey. I will love you forever...and a day!

- Stephanie Wermuth, my wonderful daughter. If it had not been for you, this book never would have happened. I love you—Mom.

CONTENTS

PREFACE

Come with me on a journey filled with the lowest of lows and the highest of highs. Each chapter will take you in unexpected directions. While reading my story, I ask that you substitute my situations with your own personal struggles. Everyone has adversities to face. I have definitely had my share and come very close to letting them defeat me. However, I learned to become a fighter and somewhat of a rebel in the process. The sheer will to fight saved my life many times because I made a choice.

This book travels through childhood abuse, a heartwarming love story, deep depression followed by suicide attempts, the onset of a horrible disease at the height of a lucrative career, losing everything to gain everything, an out-of-body experience, a glimpse of heaven, and finally, my life after being in the light of heaven. You will experience how it is possible to find the positive when faced with any negative. You will learn that *you* have a purpose to fulfill in your own life. Most important, you will realize, as I did, that you have a choice.

Chapter 1

WHAT AM I DOING?

Why are you so downcast, O my soul? Why so disturbed within me? (Psalm 42:5)

Stepping through the door was like entering a freak arena. Two guys slouched around, apparently waiting for customers (victims). Metal and ink covered their bodies, even their faces. Two others, hunched over their desks, looked up at me. Their wide eyes said they were as curious about me as I was about them. They all seemed like aliens. Scary. I turned to leave.

"Hi there!" one of them said. "How can we help you?"

Nothing. But that was a lie because I'd entered their domain. I should have run when I had the chance. When I stood at the door. Before it shut behind me. Before I got too nervous to do anything but giggle like an idiot.

What am I doing?

David's voice echoed in my mind, *Please don't do this, Roxie. It's just a phase. It will pass.* Now I was going behind his back.

What will my kids think? I was so angry when my daughter did this. Good thing my parents were deceased.

15

As far as I knew, three types of people got tattoos. Hoodlums wore skulls and tribal images. Sentimentalists wore reminders of people or the past. And bad Christians wore Bible verses and religious symbols.

Middle-aged and still a rebel, I no longer knew what to think. With my low self-esteem and my baldness, just stepping out the door was a battle with embarrassment—like those dreams where you find yourself half naked in public. And I was sick of wigs.

I came here to get covered in a new way. But it felt wrong.

Yet two anxious days later I was back, face down on a massage table with a hole for my face, watching Ed the tattoo artist's tennis shoes under his bouncing knee.

"Are you ready?" he gently asked.

"As I'll ever be." *What will people at church think? Will I catch a horrible disease?*

"Okay, here we go. Let me know if you need me to stop at any time."

Last chance to back out.

But I stayed.

The tattoo gun whirred, and the needle vibrated against my scalp, jabbing like a tiny machine gun. With much of the left side of my body already numb for years, I hardly felt the needle on some of the spots. Other places were hypersensitive and hurt so bad I thought I'd pass out—if I didn't throw up first.

Whenever Ed turned away to reload the gun, I peeked up and watched. I took note of smelling salts taped to one wall and a sink along another wall, just in case.

The needle seemed to vibrate right into the skull bone. Ed asked how I was doing, and I surprised him and the others: "It's a breeze," I lied.

"Wow, you must have a high pain tolerance."

How impressive I was. A lifetime of it had trained me well.

My mind traveled to the only time there was no pain—floating above my body, the glistening tunnel, and the infinite yellow field of God's waiting room. Heaven. The flowers under that deep blue eternity bloomed, colorful and vivid, beyond human description.

How close could Ed come to what they looked like? His work might look more like a cartoon. *I'm afraid I'll regret this, and it'll be too late.*

My nerves ran wild.

Then, "Owww!" *Can I stand this?* "Aieee!" *Buck up, Rox, and take it! You can do this…No, I can't!*

After about a half hour of teeth-clenching pain, I was sure my head was getting pulverized into hamburger. My scalp burned and my brain throbbed with a raging pulse. Occasionally Ed soaked a paper towel in a cool liquid and whisked it across my head. Oh, that felt good. "Why do you wipe my head so often?" I asked.

"To clean off the extra ink and blood."

"Blood?"

From my road out of childhood abuse to topping the corporate ladder to crawling away from suicide, I was still stubborn enough to endure anything to reach my goal.

I didn't know that my life would change yet again and find an open stage I'd never dreamed of.

Chapter 2

STICKS AND STONES

A cheerful heart is good medicine, but a crushed spirit dries up the bones (Proverbs 17:22).

The roller coaster called my life started in the eastern Michigan town of Lapeer.

When I was a toddler, I adored my father. Every morning when he left for work, I ran to the door and watched him get into his car. "Daddy, please don't go," I cried. I raised my little arms hoping he would come back to give me a hug or kiss and tell me he'd come home later to spend time with me. I waved goodbye until his car disappeared.

My mother held me and rocked me in her arms, which were like shields of armor made of love and understanding. I didn't yet know that her quiet consolation and encouragement would enable me to survive the coming years.

I just knew I wanted my daddy.

Emptiness invaded my heart as he casually drove away, not even aware that his little girl needed him and loved him so much. I just wanted a hug or a kiss or to hear him say he would miss me too and be home soon.

That never happened. He never came back to the door to say he'd be home soon or that he loved me. Never a kiss. Never a hug. Never a father-and-daughter time after work.

I often cried in my heart. *Please, Daddy, show me you care. Pick me up. Hug me. Tell me you love me.* My cry remained silent and hopeless.

As years passed, I figured this was normal. The father's job was not to show love or emotion; only the mother did that. So I thought.

And it went further.

Dad never gave me a kind word. Ever. He never even called me by name. Not once. *Speak my name, Dad, just once. Say it. Roxanne. My name is Roxanne. I'm not invisible. I'm standing right here. I'm your daughter. At least acknowledge me.* I may as well have been a ghost. He never had a single conversation with me, except to complain or yell. When he wanted me to do something, he told my mother, not me. He'd say, "Tell your daughter...."

As if I didn't exist.

Dad was raised in a spic-and-span world. Perfection was all he knew. To be anything else meant complete failure. He carried this tradition into our family. The house had to remain spotless and meticulously arranged at all times, not just because of him but also his mother, who habitually popped in unannounced to conduct the "white glove test." She always wore white gloves. I can't remember ever seeing her outside her own home without them. She would come and randomly test furniture to see if Ma was living up to her expectations of a housewife. Grandma targeted three areas of the house—the ledge of the china cabinet, the knick-knack shelf, and the top of the TV. Ma often reminded Steve and me to see that there was never any dust in those three spots.

Throughout our childhood, my brother, Steve, and I often got "the tour," in which Dad ushered us around the house to point out any imperfection we may have caused. If we hung the hand towel crooked, Dad yelled at us. One time, I made a little mark on the wall with my gold crayon. Why? Because I was a normal kid. Besides, the color was pretty, and I liked to see it on the wall. Hey, it was just a small spot, and I thought it added a bit of flair to the house. I paid for that with a belt lashing, a sentence with which I became very familiar. Another time while developing my interior design skills, I accidentally put a mark on the dining room table. *Oops.* This also got me the belt lashing. *Oh, come on, Dad. It's just a small scratch.* But that wasn't punishment enough, so it was off to the musty basement, where he tied me to a chair for hours with spiders my only companions. I was so afraid of that basement. Maybe that's why he tied me up there. He wanted to terrify me. Everything down there was creepy. The furnace creaked, clanged, and moaned. The coal room was full of big nests of spiders under their webs. Spider condominiums. The longer I had to stay there, the more my mind played tricks on me. *What's that noise under the stairs? Oh gosh, how long will he make me stay down here? I'd prefer the belt over this*—even though the belt would often miss my little butt and smack my back, leaving raised, bleeding welts.

I got the belt more than my brother did because I tended to be impish, and Steve tended to be quiet and thus favored. When Dad came after me, Steve escaped to his room in the attic. I can still picture him running upstairs and turning on his record player to drown out Dad's angry voice. He was a sweet boy and suffered in many ways similar to mine.

Despite being immaculate, our house—not home—was filled with the sounds of a blaring TV set competing with the loud frequencies of a non-stop police scanner, itself outdone by Dad's yelling. Dad *had* to know what was going on in Lapeer County at all times, so he purchased the scanner, which we couldn't afford, to hear every conversation between police on their beats and the station. It was on every single minute of every single day Dad was home. My bedroom unfortunately shared a wall with that horrid scanner. As it constantly blared, the call number permanently seared itself into my brain—KBH349. Sleep was nearly impossible, and if I dared ask Dad to turn the thing down, I got yelled at. This was one case where Ma stuck up for me and lowered the volume. She knew I needed my sleep, but that really irritated Dad.

Though the house had to remain perfect at all times, Dad's garage was always a huge mess, packed with stuff and more stuff on top of that. Whenever Mom asked Dad to clean it up, he went into a rage and screamed obscenities at her. I cried for her every time. And I never understood why the garage could be a continual mess.

His cars, which he bought one after another even though the family didn't have enough money, were his prized possessions. He took impeccable care of them, and no one else dared touch them.

One sunny day I wanted to get out of my prison-home and enjoy the freedom of a bike ride. I was proud of my bright blue Schwinn, which I had purchased with my own babysitting money. I set out to ride around the two blocks I was allowed to go at that time. Those two blocks became another world where my imagination could run free. Just two small neighborhood blocks were enough for refreshing and peaceful release. As my mind pranced, I wondered about the homes I rode past. Were they clean and sterile like ours? Or were they beautifully decorated with paintings and porcelain? Were these homes cozy and full of laughter? Did the families who lived there play games, go places, and actually eat meals together the way we did when I was little? I made up stories about each of them and imagined the peace, love, and fun those houses held within their walls. If only it could be that way at our house. If only.

But one particular bike-riding event is permanently branded into my mind. I went into the garage to get my bike and discovered Dad's car in the way. Heaps of stuff blocked every space between the car and the walls. The only way I could get my bike out was to climb on the hood of Dad's car and lift the bike handlebars up as I pulled it out. *That's right, Roxanne. Be veeeery careful. Gently now. He'll never know I was here.* I knew this would be a major infraction should he find out, but I tiptoed lightly over the hood anyway, ever so careful not to cause damage. I wanted to ride my bike—it was my "get out of jail free" pass.

I succeeded in getting my bike, and I whizzed, carefree, down the streets, the wind blowing through my long, reddish brown hair.

After returning home, I felt happy and refreshed. I loved my bedroom. It was painted my favorite color—pink. I had wanted to paint it myself, but Dad thought I would mess it up. However, when it was finished, I decorated it with pictures I painted myself. My stuffed animal collection was meticulously placed on my great-grandmother's hand-me-down bed, covered with a pink bedspread, of course. On the hardwood floor two shag rugs, also pink, lay beside my bed. All dime store stuff. One wall hosted a metal desk and shelves for studying, another wall my dresser and prized cosmetics and girlie items. Though not spectacular, I was proud that my room was picture perfect. It was my world, my happy haven.

Until Dad discovered muddy footprints on the hood of his car.

The house door opened and slammed the wall. Dad screamed, "WHERE IS SHE?" His feet stomped throughout the entire house and made their way to my bedroom. "She walked on the hood of my car!"

My peaceful mood slid into terror. Oh, how I wished I had a lock on my door, but what good would that have done against him? I needed to hide, and fast. But where could I hide in this tiny room? Under my bed would be the first place he'd look, so I crawled into the far corner of my closet and cowered behind my clothes.

The bedroom door burst open. "WHERE ARE YOU?"

Shuddering uncontrollably, I watched the shadows of his feet in the crack of light under the closet door. His footsteps scraped on the wood floor. *Maybe he won't find me in here.*

No such luck. The closet door flung open. My clothing whipped aside.

He looked ten feet tall. His eyes lit with fury. His face disfigured in pure anger. "I'm going to *kill* you! Do you know what you've *done*? You walked on my car! You stupid, stupid girl."

I quivered and cried, thinking this was it, my life was over.

But he just stared and didn't hit me. I think he was shocked at *himself* for saying he would kill me. Perhaps to him, that was punishment enough, because he left me there. I stayed in that closet for what must have been hours. It was one of the worst times he scared me, but it wouldn't be the last.

And the shadow of potential frights always loomed over me.

Like any other kid, I loved the sound of the school bell at the end of the day. Walk home, change my clothes, and enjoy playing with the neighbor kids. But the word "enjoy" never quite fit. I always had to be aware of the time. On my carefree bike rides, I still had to check, *What time is it?* Hopscotch? *Check the time.* Climbing trees in the park, *don't forget the time...I have to go!* Dad came home from work every day around 3:30 p.m., usually in a bad mood. And I needed to be home before him and out of his way. At all costs I avoided crossing his path and made sure to hide in my room, out of his sight.

But I occasionally forgot the time and was still outside when he came home. *Panic mode!* I would crawl into the house, running through my mental checklist: Did I leave a toy out or a towel crooked? Had I fed the dog, tracked anything in on my shoes, or left the TV on? Yes, Dad even checked the top of the TV to see if it was warm. If it was, he'd yell at Steve and me for using up electricity. The two of us felt as if we lived in an insane asylum. Even if the house was perfect, we still got the brunt of his bad day, hearing every sordid detail about how he hated his boss. And I didn't dare say anything about school in front of Dad. As the school's head janitor, his children had to be perfect at school too.

Mother's love for my brother and me wrapped us like a warm blanket in the cold of winter. Her dream to be a wife and mother had come true, but now that we were old enough to go to school, financial needs required her to return to work. She hated not being home when we came back from school and felt guilty whenever she had to hire a babysitter. Yet after each long workday, she tirelessly prepared a mouth-watering supper while listening to Dad's hollering.

Hearing him from the confines of my bedroom, my heart felt like a sinking rock. But I wiped away my tears and put on a smile when Mom called us for supper. We had to be good, quiet, and perfect. We ate on TV trays in front of the television set in the living room and did our best not to irritate Dad, who sat on the porch watching his own TV shows. Most kids don't like cleaning dishes, but for me, helping Mom do the dishes after supper was a privilege. She'd wash and I'd dry. We chatted the whole time, cherishing every minute we could talk freely with each other.

The quaint, old downtown of Lapeer lay walking distance from our home, and as I got a little older, I often walked there and peeked into store windows to see and dream about the things I thought I'd never have. Have them or not, strolling and skipping up and down the sidewalks, I felt like a bird released from a cage. My favorite stop was McCrory's Dime Store, where I bought penny candy. The little ringing bell on the front door, the creaky wooden floor, and the sweet smells of the store always perked my senses.

Every Friday night teens from miles around cruised the streets of Lapeer to meet each other and show off their cars. As I grew older, I joined them. Everyone meticulously followed the understood cruise route, as we drove around the town honking horns and having fun. Dad didn't care if I was home or gone. But Mom told me, "Stay away from cruising the streets. Bombing town is inappropriate for a young lady because it gives the appearance you're looking for boys, and a proper young lady wouldn't do that."

I grew skilled at lying.

Mom trusted me with the preacher's daughter, who was my best friend. But she was the one who taught me how to make excuses and get away with all kinds of mischief. Each Friday evening she picked me up for a night of fun and freedom. We prepared by stocking up on bags of penny candy, a tank of gas for her old junker, and a mouthful of giggles. And each time we made a different excuse. She rescued me so many times from my hellish life at home with Dad and replaced it with nights of so much laughter, I thought my sides would split.

But I always had to go back home. I hated the saying that all good things must come to an end. Why did I have to return to a home where Dad made sure I understood that I was a nuisance? Why did I have to be an unnecessary financial expenditure? Why did I have to hear him say, "I would have had a lot more money if you hadn't been born"?

He might as well have stabbed me.

Most of us grew up with the lie we were taught to say when other kids taunted us: "Sticks and stones may break my bones, but words will never hurt me." His verbal abuse was worse than the physical. I would have rather gotten the belt every day than hear the things he said to me. Being told I was ugly, worthless, and stupid got engrained in my mind and become my sole identity. Yet something in me, a desperate spite, chose to fight back.

Once he provoked me to the point where, without thinking, I blurted, "I hate you!"

He glared at me.

Oh no. What did I just do?

He chased me until he caught me. Then came the belt. But again his words hurt more than the bleeding welts. The cursing and put-downs were like hammers that would follow me throughout my lifetime, beating me into the ground and crushing my self-esteem. How much lower could my self-esteem go? I quickly found out.

Dad found other ways to humiliate me that I won't even describe. I became distressed with the things he said to me, the ways he touched me, the times he wanted me to change clothes in front of him. Just the way he looked at me gave me the creeps.

One day when I was in eighth grade, I made the mistake of telling my mom within earshot of Dad, "My teacher got angry at me during class for throwing a piece of paper in the wastebasket without asking for permission."

Most people would have considered it no big deal, or that the teacher had a problem. But not Dad. He came in and screamed, *"You think you're the queen bee!"* Then he went too far and grabbed me where he shouldn't have.

That was it. Something clicked in my mind and switched to autopilot. I turned into someone I'd never known before. Rage welled up from my gut. Hatred flowed out like lava from an erupting volcano. I didn't care what he did any more. This would be the *last* time I'd let him do that. I squeezed my fist, cocked my arm, and swung as hard as I could. That fist of mine smacked him square in the jaw. I could hardly believe it. I really did it. Finally.

The look on his face was priceless—wide-eyed and shocked.

With a resolve I didn't know I had, I bellowed, "That's the last time you'll ever lay a hand on me!"

And after that he never did.

As far as I knew, he didn't hit my mother, but he screamed and swore at her and called her all sorts of names. The early years were the worst. His yelling vibrated the walls. It hurt so much to hear him abuse a mom who didn't provoke it in any way. She worked a difficult job, provided for us kids, kept a clean house, cooked wonderful meals *every day*, and was a faithful wife to an impossible husband. I never saw her cry nor did I ever hear her talk back. Maybe she should have stood up to him. But even though she never did, in my eyes she was a saint, always kind and giving. She silently endured everything and kept our home life a secret. No one else, not even her own mother or best friend, knew how she suffered.

The weird thing is that on the outside we really did look like a perfect family. We could have posed for a Norman Rockwell painting—Dad, Mom, first-born son, and a daughter two years younger. But the happy painting would not carry labels of the son as Dad's prize and the daughter as Dad's burden. Dad loved hearing his son practice his squeaky saxophone but yelled at his daughter to stop practicing her squeaky clarinet. Noise from Steve's attic bedroom must have been more tolerable than noise from my room, which was right off the living room where the coveted TV and police scanner blared.

I looked up to my brother. He never stepped out of line by getting angry. He just accepted what he was given—or should I say not given. Because Dad was so meticulous about his cars that Steve was rarely given an opportunity to drive them. This was particularly frustrating to him once he got his driver's license and wanted to begin dating. I felt so sorry for him, yet he never complained.

I learned that Dad himself had been raised in cruelty, and now that I'm an adult, I can understand his behavior. His own childhood was defined by his mother's continual physical and verbal abuse, and his life seems to have been worse than ours. Grandma often locked Dad into a hope chest as a punishment, which made him claustrophobic his entire life. The saddest part is how she felt about him right after giving birth. When the nurse tried to place my father in her arms, she yelled, "Take that bastard away, I don't want him." That characterized her life-long treatment of him. He was an unwanted commodity, mistreated physically and verbally in ways I will never know.

He passed on to my brother and me what was done to him.

From my youth into adulthood I grew to habitually cheat in order to look good or gain recognition, and I lied more than ever.

Greed and hatred ran rampant through me. I later learned that my attitude and behavior were reactions to my father's abuse. It pushed me down the wrong path many times because I never felt worthy or loved.

Though I had abysmal self-esteem, I was stubborn. I learned to fight for survival. And I determined to rise above my father's janitor status. I would show him and everyone I could be successful on my own. I would rise high. I would become *the Roxinator!*

From childhood all the way through adulthood, I harbored the commitment that when my father died, I would *not* shed a tear. I made a plan: After he was buried I would go back to the cemetery and dance—yes, dance—on his grave. I hated that man.

Mom, I called her "Ma," was raised on a farm with five brothers and a sister. They were poor. Her father pastored many small Nazarene churches during her life on the farm. Two of her brothers became Nazarene pastors and her sister married one. Why Ma ever married a man like my father defies explanation, yet she endured more than fifty years with him. And she was my mentor, spiritual teacher, and best friend. She was a godly, wonderful mother, who loved me unconditionally. And I loved her. We shared our pain. And in that sharing I learned how to live and thrive, even when life felt hopeless.

She did her best to make my brother and me feel special. Every holiday became a great event, especially Christmas. She wrapped everything, even if it was a pencil. One year I got twelve pencils, each individually wrapped. Each pair of socks was individually wrapped. Though Dad didn't want to spend any money on us, at Christmas Ma made us feel like millionaires.

She spent hours and hours making Barbie doll clothes and sewed in my bedroom in the dark so as not to wake me; I was always proud whenever I saw Barbie doll clothes in a store, because what Ma created was far better. She made roast beef dinners that I'll never forget; I can still smell the steam rising from the meat and taste the dark brown gravy on the mashed potatoes. She taught me to be respectful and thankful, to be a proper young lady, and to always use correct grammar and manners. More than that, she guided and counseled me through my awkward growing up years as best as she could.

Many Sunday evenings, Ma's girlfriends would come over to our house after Sunday evening service and play games, eat snacks Ma had prepared, and talk for hours. I loved to see her happy and hear her laugh. She always looked forward to these times, and she needed them. But after her friends went home, Dad would yell at her and ask why she always had to have them over after church. It robbed all the evening's joy. Ma loved our little church and was a volunteer secretary there for many years. But Dad berated her about that too, because her spare time was to be spent taking care of him and keeping the house spotless. Ma was a beautiful woman, but her beauty seemed to die with her sinking self-esteem and fading smiles.

Poor Ma always had to wear a wig. She inherited thin hair, and it thinned further as she got older. Dad wouldn't allow her to be seen that way. So even at home on the hottest days, she always wore a wig and only removed it to bathe or sleep.

Ma neutralized Dad's negative words with positive words. Her sweetness for his bitterness made life almost palatable. She and I had tender conversations in the bathroom, where we could lock the door and be safe from Dad's criticism. I would tell her everything, how the kids teased me at school or that I was having a hard time with some of my classes.

Ma couldn't bear to see Dad abuse me, so she would retreat to another room until it was over. When the time was right and safe, she came to my room to comfort me. She didn't stop Dad from hitting me because the situation only escalated if she tried to intervene. And she didn't have it in her to fight or leave. She felt it was best to let him get his rage out of his system because things soon settled down afterward.

Her love and kindness saved me from self-destruction many times. But her love could never fully overcome Dad's torment. So I counted down the years, then the months, weeks, and days until I would graduate from high school and leave home, my prison.

Years later after I married, Ma looked at me with tears in her eyes.

I asked her what was wrong.

She choked out the words, "I'm so sorry."

"What on earth for, Ma? You're the best!"

"I'm sorry I didn't protect you when you needed me."

That was hard for both of us. She had done what to her was her best, but it rarely shielded me. Still we loved each other and felt each other's heartache.

I always feared losing her.

But it was she who lost me.

On the steps of Williams Hall, my dormitory at Olivet Nazarene University, I wept and held her tightly. I didn't want to let go of her. I worried about what life would be like for her without me there to buffer Dad's temper. With my brother having gone to Olivet two years before me, I could visualize Dad taking his frustrations out entirely on her. I felt happy to leave him but guilty to leave her. We parted, and I watched their car drive out of sight.

I could almost hear Ma crying as hard as I was. I could vicariously sense her loneliness, feeling that her job as my mother was now over. My heart physically hurt.

But I had to look ahead. Walking across campus, surrounded by red brick buildings and green grass, I thought, *Now my life will begin!*

It did and it didn't.

Chapter 3

THE LOVE CHAPTER

Beloved: I am a rose of Sharon, a lily of the valleys. Lover: Like a lily among thorns is my darling among the maidens. Beloved: Like an apple tree among the trees of the forest is my lover among the young men. I delight to sit in his shade, and his fruit is sweet to my taste. He has taken me to the banquet hall, and his banner over me is love (Song of Songs 2:1–4).

When I was little I dreamed of growing up and becoming a mom myself. I sometimes asked, "Mommy, did God pick out a boy just for me?"

She would always smile and say, "Yes, honey, God has made the perfect boy just for you."

When I was twelve I met him. He was the new kid starting seventh grade a few weeks late, and he sat right behind me. Mr. Schadel, the band director, introduced us. "Roxanne Roberts, this is David Wermuth." *Groan...okay, Roxanne, just turn around, smile, and get this over with.* Then my eyes met his. My heart thumped. A harp seemed to be playing somewhere in the background. Wow, he was cute. Kind of like Buddy Holly.

People talk lightly about love at first sight, but in my case it was true. This tall, slim twelve-year-old boy with dark curly hair, thick black-rimmed glasses, and a smile that lit up the room was going to be my husband someday. I just knew it.

I learned that David began seventh grade late because his family had just moved to Lapeer County. His father was a Nazarene pastor who relocated to the Beulah Church of the Nazarene, a little country church in Attica, five miles from Lapeer. My grandfather was one of the first pastors of this same church many years earlier. My aunts and uncles went there; my parents were married there; and my grandparents were close friends with the Wermuth family. They even referred to David's dad as their sixth son. Who would have thought? This was too good to be true, but I hoped it was meant to be.

God not only sent me this twelve-year-old boy, He also sent me a wonderful father figure—David's dad, the Reverend David E. Wermuth. I had never met another man like him. He amazed me. I thought all fathers yelled and hit their kids, but he was kind. I never saw him lose his temper or raise his voice. And he always had a positive attitude, even when he had good reason to be ticked. He was God's miraculous answer to the sea of pain and emptiness caused by my own father. I sometimes wonder how adrift my life would have been without the attention and guidance I received from him—more than he will ever know, and maybe more than I will ever know.

The first two years in band, David sat directly behind me. To sit so close to someone I adored made me tingle. Could it be possible that he felt the same way about me? Nope. I was a scrawny plain-Jane. Maybe he would see the similarities in our lives and take an interest in me. Not that either. *He's cute and I'm a geek.* I came up with a plan to get David's attention without being obvious. I attended every church-related function hoping I would run into him. But no matter how many times we ran into each other, he had the wandering eyes of a teenage boy. *Grrr...*that irritated me.

The thing I remember most about my new heartthrob was how he walked during marching band rehearsal. He was bow-legged, and his legs matched the swinging of his head as he marched along with his trumpet. Adorable! David had no idea how much I loved him. He caught the eye of another girl in seventh grade. Oh sure, it had to be the popular one—Cindy. How could I possibly compete with her? She was pretty, smart, self-confident, wore pretty clothes, and her father was a dentist. How could he? It was supposed to be me, not her. I felt the urge to pull her hair whenever I saw her. But as young romance goes, my jealousy was short lived—until the next girl caught his eye. By the time we reached high school, we knew each other well, mainly through the church. Still David had no clue of how deeply I had fallen in love with him.

But to be near David, I had to survive Mr. Schadel, the most feared teacher in the school district.

A band director in the Lapeer schools for decades, he was a perfectionist, which exacerbated a drinking problem. The drinking made him grumpy and mean spirited. My Uncle Jim had once been his student. Mr. Schadel hauled off and hit Uncle Jim one day and got a severe warning from Grandpa—and never laid a hand on Uncle Jim again. By the time I came along, Mr. Schadel only yelled and ridiculed. Lucky me. His usual behavior was to humiliate students whenever the opportunity presented itself, which was basically every day. This was his way of making us better musicians, so he said, but I think he enjoyed traumatizing us.

Mr. Schadel taught both junior and senior high, so as I progressed into high school, he continued to ridicule and humiliate me on an almost daily basis because I was a good player but couldn't count beats in the music. Mr. Schadel did not have the patience for such nonsense. I found comfort in David's saying the man was an equal opportunity ogre. But Dave's motto was: "Don't make eye contact, and for goodness sakes, don't say anything back to him. Just nod your head and smile." I could have learned from David, but the Roxinator was in the making.

Because of long hours of practice, I surpassed my upperclassmen to reach first chair clarinet. This made me a target, and I was expected to play perfectly, including solos and major parts. It also put me in a point blank firing line—an arm's length from Mr. Schadel's podium. My inability to count well made things almost impossible. He heard my every mistake, and when he did he made me play a passage of music alone in front of the entire band. When I got it wrong, as I usually did, he got so mad he showered me with expletives and broke his baton over his music stand. I wonder how many batons the school had to re-order. Perhaps I was the cause of the rising school tax in Lapeer County during my four years of high school.

I knew that if I didn't have the part just right the next day, I would get berated and put down again. On top of the abuse at home, facing this at school almost caused me to drop out of band. But I decided to fight—like the time I smacked my dad in the jaw. I was going to show this teacher that I could play and play well.

At home I practiced my parts for hours until my bottom lip split open and bled. The next day, when called out in front of the whole band to play the passage of music, I did it perfectly. *Ha! Take that!* This made him even angrier because he didn't have anything to criticize. Inside, I was laughing my head off!

Years later, Mr. Schadel had a stroke and lived his last days in a nursing home. Some thought he deserved it, but I felt sorry for him and visited him regularly. Why would I do that for such a curmudgeon? Because he taught me more than music. He unwittingly trained me to face life: If you want something, you have to work hard. You have to fight for it. That's how I succeeded in my career. During my visits with him at the nursing home, I told him about my jobs and, were it not for him, I wouldn't have gotten far. I even played my clarinet for him, and though he could no longer speak, the look on his face was admiring and grateful. I thanked him, nasty as he was, for believing in me and expecting me to do well. Of all my teachers, he impacted me the most.

I am continually reminded of these lessons because I still have a scar on the inside of my bottom lip from practicing so hard. The pain of that scar was a small price for gaining determination and discovering the love of my life.

Through most of high school David and I dated—but not each other. He still didn't have a clue. David had become popular with the girls, and I was still a plain-Jane wallflower. But we became good friends, and when he didn't have other dates for the weekend, we often kept each other company and slurped root beer at the A&W drive-in—complete with carhops. Whenever the Lapeer church held an event, we went with each other. I loved to hold his hand as we roller-skated in the couples skate. My imagination would take me to being his real girlfriend and marrying him someday.

Other outings found us attending his dad's church services at the Beulah Church of the Nazarene. One crabby old lady at that Podunk place said, "Well, that relationship will never work out. She's just too highfalutin for the pastor's son." I was practically as poor as they were! But I had the nerve to show up to church in a store-bought dress, *and* I attended Lapeer Church of the Nazarene, a small church in a small town but known in Beulah as "the city church."

Because good Nazarenes weren't allowed to go to dances, movies, bowling allies, or to swim together, we didn't have much to do. So David often took me for rides in his family's red Volkswagen Bug. We drove nearly every street of Lapeer. He even taught me how to drive and took me to a field where I couldn't run into anything. Great idea. Well, maybe not. As we jerked and bounced along, I think I drove David crazy more than I learned to drive the car. While I was trying to learn how to shift, we smelled smoke. That couldn't be good. David got out of the car and inspected it for damage. Nothing too serious. The engine just overheated from all the hay the car was collecting from the field. All seemed well—until the next day. As David's dad was driving it, the engine overheated again, seized up, and abruptly stopped. Major damage. He popped open the rear hood of the Bug and discovered the cooling fan intake totally clogged with straw. *Hmmm... How did that get there?* It was not a good day for David's dad, and it was a worse day for David after he got home from school.

Another time we skipped a boring class at school to go driving. My dad, who was running errands for the school, caught us. After his yelling, we immediately returned to school and tried to sneak back in but got caught and sent to "the bench" in the principal's office. We were "the good kids," and this was a first for both of us. The bench was in plain, humiliating view for all the students to see. On the other hand, some of the students concluded that David and I were now cool. Despite these car escapades, our families were still happy about our friendship, and I think they secretly hoped it would become more. They didn't have to wait long.

When our 1971 high school graduation finally arrived, we both realized that we would be separated for the first time in our six years of friendship. I was preparing to leave home for Olivet Nazarene University in Illinois, and David was leaving for Owosso Bible College in Michigan. He had applied for ONU, but his financial grant had not been approved, so plan B was to go where his father had attended, Owosso Bible College. Uncertainty about this separation troubled and surprised us both. Why did we *both* care so much?

Later that summer the weeklong revival at Oak Grove Campground in Lum, Michigan, was coming to a close. My girl friend and I drove into the wooded area near an old, worn-down meeting hall known as "the tabernacle." Sitting through long services on the hard wooden benches was almost unbearable. Wooden windows, propped open, let in a cool breeze, along with unrelenting mosquitos. The final service was about to take place. I felt almost frantic as I looked around and couldn't see the Volkswagen Bug. Then David came walking out of the tabernacle. He had a huge grin on his face and waved to both of us. I hoped he'd been waiting for me too. After the service David offered to drive me home. Are you kidding? Of course! We drove away in the red Bug holding hands and talked for hours that evening. Somewhere along the way David had fallen in love with me too.

Only two weeks remained before we would pack and go our separate ways. Clouds of anxiety shadowed each day. The time remaining for us to be a couple was too short. Would the separation of college end us? After all these years of dreaming, hoping, and praying, ecstasy slid into sadness.

Then David got a letter in the mail from Olivet Nazarene University. His financial papers had been misplaced, and now that they were found, the grant was approved. Whoopee! Amazing how finding one lost letter can change everything. Just like that, we set off to ONU together.

Our love continued to grow during our freshman year. We spent every moment we could with each other—and it reflected in our not-so-good grades. If I saw him across the campus lawn, I'd run toward him as if I hadn't seen him for years. Between classes we were inseparable. We'd go to the corner ice cream stand and walk hand-in-hand at Riverside State Park, talking for hours. Or we'd sit in the lobby of my dorm or student center, or walk around the campus lawns, lush with trees, flowers, and manicured shrubs. We spent hours walking together, intoxicated with each other.

The only thing that tarnished our seemingly perfect love was jealously. Mine. And it got progressively worse. Other college girls seemed so self-confidant, pretty, and smart. Who was I? I had been told all my life I was incompetent, plain, and stupid. Even after getting away from Dad, the thoughts haunted me and ravaged me every day. I couldn't stop believing I was unworthy of anything—even to live.

I reinforced this every time I looked in the mirror, where my thin, baby-fine hair lilted in strands under the Illinois humidity. I inherited the thin hair from my mother, who had always worn a wig. Since childhood I had ached for thick, long, bouncy hair. My favorite fairytale was *Rapunzel,* which I read over and over until the book was in tatters. I wished for thick hair at every birthday and upon every falling star. Instead I had to settle for this thin stuff that nearly exposed my skull. Closing my eyes, I often dreamt of those long locks and repeated to myself the line, "Rapunzel, Rapunzel, let down your hair."

I convinced myself that David would find someone smarter and prettier. But I couldn't stand the thought of losing him. Instead of trying to hold on to him by being sweeter and more caring, I became bitter. I questioned his every move. I made his life miserable. He must have truly loved me because any other guy would have run for his life.

I had suicidal thoughts on a regular basis. One day the jealously rooted in my low self-esteem became too much, and I concluded I would never be good enough for David.

Alone in my dorm room, I took an arsenal of medications stored in my closet—everything I could get my hands on. Then I lay on my bed to die. My vision blurred and my body ached. I thought of my mother and my brother. I wondered if I would go to hell because I was killing myself. *How painful is dying? Or will I become a drooling zombie?* My stomach began to hurt. The room spun. My whole insides writhed in pain. I ran to the dormitory bathroom and vomited up all the pills. I couldn't decide if I was relieved or sad. But it seemed like a sign that I shouldn't attempt that again.

Unfortunately, this attempt didn't change anything in my life. I was still insanely jealous and kept having regular thoughts of ending my life. I was convinced David would turn to someone else. I guess I was trying to push him away before he would take the chance to leave me. Despite my attitude and behavior, David remained loyal to me and tried to be patient and understanding. I didn't need to worship saints; I had one as a boyfriend.

Winter brought the annual revival meeting at the college church, where we went to every evening service. David was letting temptations get the better of him, I reacted, and we had a colossal argument. I decided to break up, and it devastated him.

He told me that if I didn't go to the last revival service with him, he wouldn't go. I was still angry and had no intention of getting back together with him. But I was worried about him and wanted him to go to the meeting for his own good. So I forced myself to go with him.

We were both tense and didn't even speak to each other as we walked to the church. We arrived so late that the only place to sit was in the last row of the balcony. Perched in the far corner of this mass of people, I felt as if it were just the two of us. Yet David appeared deeply affected by what the speaker said.

When the guy finished, he invited people to pray at the altar. David stood and descended the stairs. *Oh my.* He was shy, and to make this long walk from the back of the balcony *waaaay* down to the altar was a huge step for him. I watched him kneel. I watched him pray. I watched his shoulders shake as he cried. He had *never* done this kind of thing before.

Maybe God was healing both him and our relationship.

I started praying for him, and as I did, I sensed God speak to me.

David will be my servant in the church.

Okay. That made sense. But then...

David will ask you to marry him. Say yes.

"Huh?" Whoa. Where'd that come from? Did I make it up? No, it was too clear.

Maybe I imagined it. No, it was totally out of my experience as well as my character.

It was as if God proposed to me on David's behalf. Too weird. But weird enough for me to get past my anger.

I shivered, but not from the cold. I waited anxiously for David to return to the balcony and see if he would really say this stuff to me. The minutes dragged like hours.

After he prayed for what seemed like half an eternity, he returned. And he looked happy. He told me what God had in store for him—servant in the church. Then he said, "There is something else too."

"I know."

He stared at me.

"And yes, I will."

His mouth dropped open.

Yes, God proposed for David.

We sat in the balcony and embraced for what seemed like the other half of eternity. And I didn't want it to end. But the maintenance guys were locking up the building.

We called home to our parents and cried as we told them what happened. Instead of worrying that we were so young, they were all happy for us. In just six months we would be married—and we would still be eighteen.

To this point, this night was the happiest time of our lives.

I never told anyone until now, but as I was still seated in that balcony during the revival, hearing God speak to me, there came another voice.

It carried a dark presence and felt like a living creature, creepy and evil. It chilled me to the bone and made my skin crawl. I didn't know whether it was my imagination, but I doubt it. These are the words I clearly heard in my mind's ear: *"You think your life will be easy since God called you two to be together. But I promise you, it won't. I will make it as hard as I can for you."*

Chapter 4

RISING AND CRASHING

Now listen, you who say, "Today or tomorrow we will go to this or that city, spend a year there, carry on business and make money." Why, you do not even know what will happen tomorrow. What is your life? You are a mist that appears for a little while and then vanishes (James 4:13–14).

"I know I can climb higher," I often said to myself. And for a while I did, even after having children.

Unlike my brother I had to pay for my college education. Dad said it wasn't important for a girl to go to college. I hated him for that.

But I loved David, and we married between our freshman and sophomore years of college. I soon dropped out in order to work and put him through school. He made a career in children's protective services. I never got a degree. And I could only wonder how much higher I might have climbed with one.

Against Ma's best advice, I wanted to get pregnant so I could have a stronger hold on David because of my rising insecurity and jealously. At least that worked. I didn't have the time or energy to be jealous anymore.

I gave birth to two girls, Stephanie and Sara. I adored them and was overly protective. I cherished my time with them by reading bedtime stories and rocking them to sleep. I wanted to give them the world and be a mother like my mom was to me, but I never lived up to Ma's example. I made one mistake after another. I returned to work as a respiratory therapist after a short six-week leave of absence and put Stephanie in the hands of a babysitter I barely knew.

The blaring alarm sounded at four in the morning. Wake up, get dressed, pack the diaper bag, get Stephanie fed and dressed, pack the car, *don't forget the baby*, leave home by five sharp! Drive to the baby sitter's house, drop off the diaper bag and baby supplies, *don't forget the baby*, drive across town to Riverside Hospital, clock in by six a.m.

After Stephanie we waited six years before Sara was born so I could have the choice to return to work part time or stay at home. I missed my job and returned to work after a four-month leave of absence. David and I decided to schedule opposite shifts to minimize her time in daycare. Good for the child; not good for the marriage.

After eight years at that hospital, I was invited to work for a home health care company, checking on people who had respiratory problems. I made the change and found I loved working with patients in their own homes. The company eventually moved me into sales, where I called on local physicians and explained the benefits of using our company. I was good at sales and marketing, and I liked the competitiveness—enough to claw my way to the top.

I would not spend the rest of my life feeling beaten-down and worthless. I'd prove to my dad and my family that I could make something of myself even though I didn't receive a degree.

To climb even higher, I took a leap into radio and landed a sales job at a top radio station in Flint, Michigan—WCRZ. I did well there but eventually looked for a bigger challenge.

Television. But I didn't have a clue about television, so I went to a library and read everything I could about it. After six weeks of calls and interviews with an NBC affiliate station, I had a final interview with the general station manager in mid-Michigan.

I couldn't believe I had the nerve to do this. *What am I doing here? I'm just a country girl from a small town.*

I sat before the ornate wooden desk of a chieftain in a dark suit and cufflinks who fired question after question. I felt like a duck in a shooting gallery. Behind me sat three people who had previously interviewed me, their pencils scratching notes the entire time. If they meant to intimidate me, it worked. I grew painfully aware of every word I said and every move of my fidgeting body.

The station manager finally looked straight at me and asked, "Roxanne, do you think you could sell *anything*?"

"Given the proper information about a product, yes. I could sell sand in the desert." *That was arrogant. I shouldn't have said it.*

"Hmm. Anything?

"Yes, anything."

"Okay." He picked a glass ball off his desk and handed it to me. "Sell me this."

A paperweight. *What can I say about a paperweight? It's just a round piece of glass.* Time seemed to stop as I tried to speak. My mind raced, heart pounded, and nothing came out of my mouth. *Oh my. Just say something. Anything.*

The station manager stared at me. The three behind me waited. An eternity trudged by in seconds.

"My name is Roxanne Wermuth. I'm with Paperweight, Incorporated, and I'm here to tell you how this simple object can benefit your life. As nicely stacked as those papers on your desk may be, it'll only take a gust through an open door or the brush of an important client's coat to scatter them across the floor. Think of the embarrassment." I held the ball toward him. "Look closely. It's finely crafted and beautifully designed, a good conversation starter. Here, hold it."

The station manager put his hands up and chuckled. "In all the years I've been doing this, I've given people staplers, tape dispensers, pencils, you name it. You're the first person who's taken right off and sold it to me. That'll be all, Mrs. Wermuth."

I was excused, and they said they'd call me. *Yeah, right.* I walked away, wishing someone would put me out of the misery of wondering whether I got the job that I had no chance of getting anyway. Half way out the door, I heard the secretary. "Mrs. Wermuth! Mrs. Wermuth! Could you come back in?"

I wondered if they would ask why I wasted six weeks of their time when I had no formal education in either marketing or sales. I probably deserved it. But when I walked in, they were all smiling. The station manager told me he had never done this before—he hired me on the spot. I tried to look dignified as I walked out but jittered with excitement when I reached my car.

I called David and Mom and Dad right away. Dad was not impressed. I couldn't even get him to watch the station after I got the job. "Hey, Dad. I wrote and produced some local commercials. Don't you want to see them?" No answer. Would there ever be a time he'd take pride in his daughter? As I had my entire life, I longed for the slightest acknowledgement of my accomplishments. *Just love me!* But I only got cold silence. I had to settle with myself that my dad's approval could not—must not—matter to me. I could never become my brother, the favored son, who followed my Dad's career by working for the same school district as a custodian.

I clenched my teeth. I'd show him anyway. Just to spite him.

My fighting spirit took over.

At Channel 5 I sold airtime and produced commercials. I spared nothing in my pursuit of success. At first I didn't fit in with my coworkers. They were sophisticated, knowledgeable, and dressed in fine business attire. I was none of that. I was so awkward that my sales manager referred to me as "the pansy." And I was. I felt as though I were back in high school as the plain-Jane band geek. So I determined to fit in—at any cost. I drifted far from the Christian life I had been taught and joined them in drinking at bars after work, getting drunk and driving home, joking and drinking at company parties. But I knew it wasn't right. I sensed an inner struggle even as I succeeded in matching the flashy reputations of the movers and shakers in this fast-paced corporate world.

Greed and pride consumed me. I made poor choices that came with serious consequences. Some choices hurt my co-workers, who had helped train me and considered me a friend. I skimmed the cream of the crop off the client list to my favor and had a local business call the station to request a change from another representative to me so I could receive the commissions. I knew better than to do that, but making money and being number one was more important.

Other choices hurt my marriage. I chastised David for not working as hard or making as much money as I did. After all, I had worked to put him through college. He had the degree, not me. I felt cheated and angry. *Why doesn't he have the drive to move up like I do? Why is he content to have a job and not use his degree to be a mover and shaker too?* So I became even more self-absorbed. That meant spending less time with him and adding stress on myself. I was often cruel to him and inflicted on him an unpredictable trigger temper. David's career in children's protective services wasn't good enough for me at that time. I wanted *him* to climb even higher. But he was content and happy to protect children. I eventually realized he was right. David would become one of the best in his field, and people loved him. Years later at his retirement, he received a plaque stating: "A hundred years from now it will not matter what my bank account was, the sort of house I lived in, or the kind of car I drove—but the

world may be different because I was important in the life of a child"
(Forest Witcraft).

My two girls got the same treatment. They were now teenagers,
and their moodiness and pickiness wore on my nerves. Why couldn't
they just be perfect and quit causing me stress? I was important. And
I did *not* have the time or energy at the end of the day to put up
with them. So I yelled at them and hit them just as my father had
done to me.

His shadow wouldn't go away. Since childhood I had always felt
like ugly, stupid rubbish. I only took up space—even now as an adult
who'd become a corporate climber.

But something new was happening: Other men were attracted
to me. This left me flabbergasted. For a while I struggled with this,
yet I indulged in it and hurt David terribly. I did the unthink-
able—cheated on him and broke his heart. What had I become? He
deserved someone better.

Yet I threw my wrongs back at him and accused him of the very
things I was doing. Jealously again ruled my life and became like a
weapon against him and a shield against admitting my own realities. I
grilled David every night when he got home from work. I wouldn't even
let him look at a *TV Guide* because it had pictures of pretty women.
David went his own way and grew distant. My marriage and family life
spun out of control to the point that we separated for six months.

The anxiety I generated landed me in a counselor's office. A lot.
I found how critical and influential is a father's love for his daughter.
Without the love of a father, and in my case the abuse I got instead, *I
had become my father.*

But I had what was important—recognition, money, a BMW in
the driveway, and a dream house with a garden that graced brochures
of local landscapers. And my superficial life went on.

I never intended to share these things with anyone. They almost
caused me not to tell my story because I didn't want to embarrass

my family, especially David's side. But I saw that people needed to know who I really was. I wish I could go back and erase the ugliness. Sometimes David and I discuss the past and acknowledge how blessed we are to have made it through those days. Two important lessons always come through: Fathers, love your kids. And couples, fight for your marriage—don't give up easily. I never want to see that kind of pain in David's eyes and vow never to hurt him that way again.

After nearly seven years with Channel 5, a headhunter recruited me to work sales and marketing at a nationwide company called ABC Home Health Care. It was the hardest change of my career. My job was to call on 400 doctors in four geographical zones of eastern Michigan. Every week I worked a different zone. Required to call on a minimum of ten physicians per day, I pushed myself to call on fourteen to seventeen, working from morning to late afternoon, usually without lunch.

Though I worked just as hard as I had at NBC, I determined I would become a better person. Disgusted with myself over the narcissist I had turned into and how I had treated my family, friends, and co-workers, I determined to change. I wanted to be successful on my own merits, not false impressions or cheating. My previous commitments had failed, but with this one I held on.

I struggled and occasionally faltered as I reconciled with my husband and daughters, changed my attitude toward co-workers and clients, and quit lying and cheating. People wondered what happened to the old Roxanne. Instead of seeing coworkers as obstacles in my climb to the top, I saw them as teammates—friends, helpers, and people to whom I now showed compassion. I took a genuine interest in prospects and clients. Instead of relying on beauty, flirting and lying, I returned to my mother's roots of humility, honesty, and respect.

I was truly happy for the first time in years. I seemed to be finally getting my life together. David grew proud of me for the effort and creativity I poured into my job. We grew close again, no longer living two separate lives like passing ships.

ABC Home Health Care gave me the smallest office in Michigan, which was about to close if it didn't do any better within one year. I felt cheated that the company hadn't told me this before I took the job. I was disappointed, because I'd been making a lot of money at Channel 5. But then the medical company offered me almost double that salary, and more than David ever made as a children's protective service worker.

This became my dream job. I worked long hours and dressed professionally or casually relative to what zone I visited. Two zones were very country; two were big city. I was especially kind to the receptionists, because they were the gatekeepers. I kept notes of doctors' and receptionists' names, marriages, children, and birthdays. I never took anything for granted. For every referral I sent a thank-you note. I took lunches and donuts to offices—all the things a busy doctor would like. The company had 250 sales reps nationwide, and I became one of the leaders. This miniscule office grew to the largest in the state. Every year the company held a national sales conference at the home office in Atlanta. After the first year people sought me out for advice, and I started traveling and doing how-to-sell classes.

Then my life went off a cliff.

June 1994, a sunny 8:30 a.m., I walked into a Lapeer doctor's office for the day's first business appointment. I felt oddly tired and garbled my words. But I brushed it off.

On the way out I ran into the doorjamb. I bumped into the doorframe of the car and fell into the seat. I couldn't figure out what was wrong with me. I probably just needed to wake up, so I got a cup of coffee at McDonalds.

I went on to a brand-new foster care home for the elderly, where they gave me a tour. I couldn't keep my balance, and I repeatedly reached for the walls to stabilize myself. I figured the owner of the building would suspect I'd been drinking, and it was only 9:00 a.m. I struggled down the steps to my car, when my left toes started tingling. Driving 500 miles a week usually put my right toes to sleep because they were on the gas pedal or brake—but never my left. As I drove, the tingling spread to my foot then my leg, until the entire left side of my body grew numb and tingling.

I went home and called my doctor.

"Roxanne, you need to go to the emergency room."

"That's silly. I feel fine. I just have a little numbness and tingling. Can't I just pop into your office and get a pill or a shot so I can go back to work?"

"No. This sounds serious. Get going."

The Lapeer General Hospital emergency parking lot was full, so I parked at a church across the street. When I got out of my car, I could hardly lift my leg. I dragged it behind me and thought, *I must look like the Hunchback of Notre Dame.* Several nurses stood with a gurney in front of Emergency. *Wow, there must be accident victims coming in.*

I got to the door and they asked, "Are you Roxanne?"

"Yes."

"Get on this gurney."

They were waiting for me! *Oh boy. This is not good.*

They wheeled me into a room and hooked me up to all kinds of monitors.

"What's going on?"

"Your doctor called. He thinks you may have had a stroke."

Who on earth has a stroke at age forty?

I called David. He came. And held me as my mind careened through a maze of disbelief and fear.

During a week in the hospital, I lost my ability to walk. My speech grew more garbled, as if I were drunk. I lost most of my vision to where I could only see five feet. But even that was blurry, and I couldn't tell who or what I was looking at. My muscles went into spasms. I struggled merely to think. My body seemed to have a will of its own and refuse to cooperate with my mind. The doctor finally said, "I'm afraid you haven't had a stroke."

Whew! Glad to hear that.

"So far, your tests are normal, but it is very possible you have a white matter disease."

"Speak English!"

"We think you may have multiple sclerosis. But we're not sure."

Oh. No big deal. As if he were ordering a pizza.

Multiple sclerosis.

No!

I only knew one person who had MS, a doctor who once worked at Lapeer General Hospital where I had worked. He was now in a wheelchair, totally paralyzed. He could talk only if he strained, and he could not feed himself.

I lost it. My body convulsed. I could not accept this. I was successful and independent. I had a husband to care for and two daughters to raise. This could not happen to me. No one in my family had anything like this.

I screamed and yelled, "Take it back!" *Rewind. Take those words back as if none of this happened.* Those two words, *multiple sclerosis*, would change my life forever. I knew it, but I wouldn't accept it. "Take it back, take it back, take it back!"

Then, as reality set in, I begged David to let me die.

Everything I had, everything I was, everything I dreamed of hit a wall. Crashed. Scattered like bits of junk to be swept into the trash.

Two nurses rushed in. I heard the doctor say "valium" and "calm her down quick." They added the medication to my IV bag and stood around the bed while it dripped in and my screams turned to whimpers. The doctor looked at me without expression. "There's nothing I can do. You may end up paralyzed. We just don't know."

I felt as if his words covered me under a white sheet.

"On the other hand," he continued, "I'm not sure. I *think* you have multiple sclerosis, but your symptoms could come from job-related stress and all be in your head."

"In my head?" *You don't know me.*

This man did not inspire confidence. To add to the experience, my roommate was a young mother of two noisy, hyperactive children. I was in no mood for this nonsense. Her doctor, an infectious disease specialist—red flag!—came into the room and told her, "It's possible you may have AIDS and tuberculosis. We're running the tests now." *Ummm…aren't AIDS and tuberculosis infectious diseases?* Then he said harshly, "This is the price you've paid for being a prostitute in Detroit." I tried and failed to feel sorry for her because I was too afraid of getting infected with TB. Soon the girl was moved into isolation.

My next roommate jolted me awake with a midnight arrival. The orderlies flipped on the lights and clanged her bed against mine as they passed, then clanged against furniture and monitors. They asked her questions and took her vitals. Finally they finished and turned off the lights. Twenty minutes later they jolted me awake again. Lights back on, I overheard the nurses talking about measuring the distance the redness had traveled on her leg. Then they checked both our blood pressures. *Whatever.* Back to sleep. Twenty minutes later the whole thing happened again. *Are you kidding me?* One nurse said the woman had "a flesh-eating disease." *What?* I had heard about this on the news. It was highly contagious. Shouldn't *she* be in isolation too? They had just used the same blood pressure cuff on her as they used on me. Sleep deprivation, feeling sick, possible MS—I went over the edge. Roxanne got a-n-g-r-y.

At two in the morning I demanded they call my husband to come and get me. They said they couldn't do that without my doctor's release, and they refused to call him in the middle of the night over a hysterical patient. I struggled out of bed, away from my flesh-eating diseased roomie and into the hallway, where I found a wheelchair. I plopped down and rolled to the visitor's lounge to sleep. Great—that's where all the nurses took their breaks. The next morning the night shift reported my behavior, which surprised everyone who knew me from my past employment there. The friendly, easygoing person had morphed into a riotous patient. Everyone has a breaking point.

The doctor came and scribbled a note that I could return to work. No other treatment or medication.

Return to work? I could hardly walk and couldn't see.

His stethoscope hung like a necklace. Doctors' jewelry. All of his medicine useless to me now.

"Good-bye," he said and walked out the door.

That's it? I'd worked with countless doctors, and none matched the jerk status of this one.

Hours after returning home, muscles all over my body seized up so much I could hardly breathe. I did *not* want to go back to Lapeer Hospital. I asked David to take me to Crittenton Hospital in Rochester Hills, an hour away.

On the way I said, "David, promise me…you won't let them… put me on…a ventilator…That would make me…so angry…I will not live that way…I'd rather die…Promise me."

He reluctantly agreed.

As we drove I kept thinking, *Who's going to do my hair?* David certainly can't style my pitiful hair. Even I had difficulty. And how will I coordinate my wardrobe? The biggest crisis of my life, and I fretted about my hairstyle and clothing.

I stayed at Crittenton for two weeks and got a clear diagnosis that I indeed had MS. But this doctor gave me hope that it wasn't necessarily a death sentence. I might even have the kind of MS that goes into remission. But no such luck. I learned I had chronic progressive MS, one of the worst types. It would never go into remission but would be with me, and get worse, the rest of my life.

Death sounded better.

The doctor put me on 1000 milligrams of steroids a day for thirteen days. It was like pumping Drano into me. It stung and ate away my veins. With every injection they had to find a new vein. My face puffed up into a "moon face," I gained weight, and my personality turned crazy. I either talked nonstop or got angry.

Despite all that I still did business from my hospital bed. I hand wrote notes to the four hundred doctors I worked with, telling them I had MS but was coming back to work. To my surprise, I received a mountain of flowers, cards, candy, and phone calls.

Multiple sclerosis (meaning many scars) is an inflammatory disease where your own body's immune system attacks itself. It originates in the brain and spinal cord, causing scar tissue to develop on the nerves and block neurotransmitters. This creates signal disruptions to the body, leading to numbness and tingling, muscle weakness, pain, spasms, loss of balance, digestive complications, cognitive difficulties, depression, vision and speech impairment, extreme fatigue, and paralysis. There is no known cure. MS is not contagious, and no one seems to know what causes it. Over the years, it seems to have become more common, suggesting possible links to the environment or even childhood illness. MS comes in several varieties. If you're going to have it, the best type would be Remitting and Relapsing MS, which can go into remission for years.

My type, chronic progressive, is with me as a daily reminder I will never be the same again. The scars (also known as plaques or lesions) continue to develop in my brain. In the beginning, the doctors could count them—two, then five, then seven. Now, my MRIs just say "numerous." In the beginning, I thought I would lose my mind from the tingling alone. Whenever someone bumps my left side, I want to scream. For example, if your arm falls asleep you get that tingling sensation, and if you bump your arm, you know just how awful it feels. I feel that way every day on my entire left side.

The doctor asked me if I was ready to stop working.

I just wanted a pill to cure me. I blew up at him. "Don't you tell me to stop working! You don't understand my finances. You don't have a kid in college." I seethed. "I finally found the perfect job and am making the kind of money I want. And you're suggesting I give it all up?"

His chair squeaked as he leaned back and crossed his arms. He smirked and shook his head. "You think if you work hard enough, you'll work MS out of your system. Everyone thinks that, but if you keep up at this pace, I guarantee you'll end up in a wheelchair soon."

I did not want to hear this.

"What's more important, your family or your career?"

"My career."

He displayed his sympathy smile and nodded his head. "It doesn't work that way, Roxanne."

I took a four-month leave of absence from the medical company. I trained myself to do things I'd always taken for granted—walk, speak, drive a car. With cognitive impairment I had to re-remember names, faces, sales presentations, even spelling. I felt stupid, although now I had a good reason. Then I went back to work.

But I soon realized my doctor was right. The more I tried to work MS out of my system, the more fatigued I became, which made the symptoms worse. At the end of each day I limped badly. But I didn't want anyone to know, so I stayed in my car filling out my charts until everyone else left. I limped as fast as I could to the building and held my hand to the walls to stabilize myself as I scurried to my chair. Someone must have seen me because after I had been back four months, my sales manager was assigned to ride with me and see if I was able to work with MS. I was determined he would not see me limp. He rode with me all day, and we visited nineteen doctors. *He* was tired and didn't know how I did it. The fact is, I couldn't. It took me three days to recuperate.

I couldn't go to the annual corporate sales meeting by myself, so my husband got special permission to go with me. He witnessed how many of the 250 sales people looked for "*the* Roxanne." They would ask me, "What do you do that makes you so successful?" And I told them about hard work and attention to the personal touch.

David was amazed to see all those sales people seeking me out for advice. I felt especially proud because I had never finished college. *Take that, Dad.*

Then one day my office manager asked me to meet him at one of my assigned hospitals. "The sooner the better," he said.

Uh-oh. This can't be good. As I waited in the hospital cafeteria, my coffee cup trembled every time I brought it to my lips. The hospital personnel in their blue scrubs talked and laughed, while I hung in the balance like a dead leaf about to drop off its tree. And fall I did. My manager came and said, "Roxanne, this is going to be one of the hardest things I've ever done." He paused. Then launched into an obviously rehearsed speech: "I've talked with corporate, and we think you need to go on a medical leave—not that you're not doing your job. You're exceeding all expectations. But you are a potential liability to the company. You drive five hundred miles a week. You get in and out of your car all day long. With the possibility that you could hurt yourself or get into a car accident, we think it would be a liability to us and a detriment to you. As much as I hate to do this, we need to put you on a medical leave."

Silence.

I cried. He cried.

He cleared his throat. "I'm going to tell you something in confidence, and you have to promise me you'll keep it to yourself."

I nodded.

"I've just received word that instead of our two-year disability plan with a small percentage of our salary, the company is going to a five-year disability plan with 60 percent of our salary. If you can just hang in here for three months, you can get into this new plan." He hunched toward me like a coach with a secret play. "I want you to work as much as you can from the office. Try to drive as little as possible. In the meantime, I'm going to send you a new recruit to train. The company is going to think you're training this person for another office. But you're actually training your replacement. This will give you an extra three years of income at double what you would have made on the old plan."

God was taking care of me.

The new recruit came along. He didn't know I was training him to replace me—until the very end. I gave him all my files. "Take good care of my doctors, my receptionists, and my nurses."

I cried. He cried.

The company threw a huge party for me, and the CEO flew up from Georgia. My whole family came. I got all the kudos

I could have asked for. My husband saw what I'd been doing. Even my father saw how successful I'd become—but of course he wouldn't acknowledge it.

I'd made it to the top: Perfect job. Highly successful. Everything I'd ever wanted. Happy marriage. Good kids.

Now my life was over. Kicked in the teeth. I had worked so hard for everything—only to lose most of it. "God, why did You let this happen to me? What did I do wrong?"

Chapter 5

TO DIE OR TO LIVE

O Lord, do not rebuke me in your anger or discipline me in your wrath. Be merciful to me, Lord, for I am faint; O Lord, heal me, for my bones are in agony. My soul is in anguish. How long, O Lord, how long? Turn, O Lord, and deliver me; save me because of your unfailing love (Psalm 6:1–4).

Dying can get in the way of living. But can living get in the way of dying?

The first year of multiple sclerosis was terrible, not just for me but also for my entire family. I was too ambitious for this. Too independent. Too proud. MS was an embarrassment. My appearance was important, and I would lose my dignity. Multiple sclerosis would disguise me like an ugly Halloween costume. The go-getter, ladder-climber Roxanne would be buried under a pitiful disabled woman in a wheelchair. My new identity.

I was bitter.

I wanted to continue to be the person I'd made myself. And I didn't want help.

I was so scared.

I cried. I yelled. I wanted to give up. I started thinking, *Lord, just let me die.* I begged my husband, "Please help me die." Every time I developed a new symptom, suicidal thoughts flooded my mind.

Convulsions and tremors came and went without warning. A paradoxical numbness and hypersensitivity engulfed the entire left side of my body. I couldn't bear to step on the smallest speck of sand. Yet at the same time, I couldn't feel my left side and sometimes my right. A small bump to my arm could set off an involuntary jerk, making me spill or drop what I was carrying or even fall. Any loud noise would nearly scare me to death. It's called the "startle factor," and David grew quite familiar with it. If he entered a room where I was and he merely spoke a word, I screamed—which in turn scared him to near death. There was no longer any such thing as walking straight and normal. To this day, if pulled over by the police, I would never pass the sobriety test of walking a straight line because the world always feels as if it were tilted. Weird as all this is, it's MS. It has stayed with me, and it's not for sissies.

I had to relearn how to use my hands, how to walk, and how to live with this invisible thief that was pilfering my life.

I could not bear the symptoms and saw no way to cope.

So I made up my mind: I would be miserable the rest of my life. Give in and give up. The previous Roxanne, so independent and proud, with a Type A personality, obsessed about a beautiful home, and a hard-working ball of fire with energy to spare, would vanish. I became a sissy.

To escape my emotional pain and anger, I often went up to Mackinaw, in northern Michigan, where I stayed with my Aunt Barb and Uncle Fred, who owned four motels there. Uncle Fred could cheer the lowest of lows. He was a wonderful source of endless laughter in the wake of my disaster. I don't know if they ever understood why I went up there by myself, but they probably knew it had something to do with my physical difficulties and depression. One year, I got so depressed and upset that I took off at 11 p.m. and didn't get there until 2:30 a.m. This kind of thing happened at least once a year after that. Each time David worried about where I was and if I was all right. He'd call me on my cell phone, but I wouldn't answer. I thought he was better off living a normal life without the burden of taking care of me. I wasn't angry with him. I was angry with myself. When I returned home I found lovely letters that he'd written and left in the kitchen for me to read. The letters always said, "Please come home to me, we'll figure this all out together. Everything will be all right. Just please come home. I love you, and that will never change."

But all that wasn't enough to pull me back from thinking my life was over.

Things got worse when I learned about hidden troubles during the past rough patches of my marriage. The old feelings of being ugly, stupid, and worthless overwhelmed me again. I was convinced David would find someone better, and the thought of losing him was too much.

Once again I got it in my head to end my life. This time, however, I took my faith more seriously and figured if I committed suicide, hell might be high on the destination agenda. So I wondered how I could end my life without committing suicide. I found a way: I would just stop eating. I already tended not to eat whenever I was stressed, which was most of the time. And eating was the only thing I felt I could control. Death by starvation would take me out guilt free. When I became too malnourished, my heart would simply stop beating. I called this "Nazarene suicide," because if I starved to death as a good Nazarene, I would go to heaven, because starvation can be a natural cause of death.

So for an entire year, anorexia became my new best friend. After the first three days, the hunger pangs subsided, and it became surprisingly easy to starve myself. I had no desire to live. This once-healthy 5-foot 7-inch woman dropped to a skeletal 103 pounds.

One day at a shopping mall, I met my best friend, the pastor's daughter—the one with whom I had escaped the house and cruised around town. She and I had often talked on the phone, but we hadn't seen each other in more than a year. She was shocked at my gaunt appearance and walked with me into a clothing store. When I took a dress into a fitting room, she came in with me.

As I changed, she said, "Look at yourself in the mirror!"

"What?"

"I mean, really. Look at yourself. See what you're doing."

Then I saw myself through her eyes. My jaw dropped. For the first time I grasped the reality of what I was doing to myself. I looked so old. So ugly.

She told me exactly what she thought: I would indeed go to hell, because starving myself was a willful desire to commit suicide. True or not, that woke me up, and I started forcing myself to eat.

My dream house had become a nightmare. I could barely walk, and this house became an obstacle course. When entering the front door, I had to either go down stairs into the living area, or up stairs to the bedrooms. I struggled every day to make do, but falling down the stairs became the new norm and sometimes David had to carry me into the bathroom because my wheelchair was too wide to fit through doorways. For a time, I just slept downstairs on the sofa. There was no adapting it to make this home handicap accessible. Depression set in again. We were 40 years old, and the house was almost paid off. Did we start all over now? We had to.

So we shopped real estate. After not liking any land I saw, we finally looked at the farmland once owned by my grandfather, John

Mellish, where my Uncle Paul had also lived. I loved that old farm, and if I was going to be forced to move, there was no other place on earth I'd rather live.

When I was young, Mom would drop me off at the farm on the weekends. Before the car even stopped, I jumped out because I was so excited to see Uncle Paul. I could always find him because of his constant whistling. I was his little shadow, and he always had time for me. He showed me how to milk the cows, slop the pigs, and gather eggs from the chicken coop. He even played games with me and took me to local stores or just for a ride in his truck. I adored him, lived in awe of him. He was the best part of my entire childhood.

And now I was back, maybe for good.

The 311-acre farm had since been parceled out and sold. I found a 13-acre parcel that included a creek with a bridge built by Uncle Paul. I told the owner my story and asked if he would sell. This elderly man was a close friend of my grandfather and told me he could have sold this property over a dozen times, but it hadn't felt right—until now. When he learned I was John Mellish's granddaughter, he even lowered the price.

I designed the house myself, a totally handicap-accessible place that didn't look like it. But how could we pay off an expensive specialty home at the age of 40 with me not working? I couldn't sleep, couldn't stop worrying. But God spoke to me and told me not to worry; it was in His hands. In the process of building, I received an unexpected inheritance, and years later an inheritance from my father enabled us to pay off the house. God's promise never fails. All over our home we have decorations and plaques that read, "As for me and my house, we shall serve the Lord."

About five years after receiving the diagnosis of MS, I had a major flare up, what's called an "exacerbation." David and I were camping with his parents on a very hot day. Heat is an enemy of MS. David and Dad Wermuth were off fishing when I felt my muscles lose control. Weakness slithered through my body, I grew dizzy, and spasms started in. I felt too embarrassed to let my mother-in-law see what was coming but too scared to be alone. She insisted on staying until someone found David and then witnessed my jerking and thrashing about. Later she told me she was glad to witness the truth because Roxanne-the-fighter had always minimized the problem.

To me, being a fighter meant not letting anyone see my weaknesses. I hated that she saw this. I hated that I couldn't hide it. I hated that I was losing the old *me*. As often happened, I vacillated between anger and fear, striving and quitting. Besides the depression normally brought on by MS, my inner conflict drove me past my combative instincts and into deep despair.

I returned to the hospital for a week, where, instead of a view of lakes and trees, I got machines and tubes. David enjoyed the vacation by driving three hours every day to visit me at the hospital.

At first I couldn't walk, and the spasms and tremors, dizziness, vision impairment, and depression were unbearable. My mind set out to do ordinary things, but when I tried, my body didn't cooperate. If I wasn't fixated on death, I was throwing things across the room.

Doctors put me on IV steroids again, which added new symptoms. I was always hungry and crawling out of my skin with anxiety. Being confined to a hospital bed and relying on nurses to care for me was like returning to infancy. And I couldn't stop feeling sorry for myself. As I lay in that bed, I pondered the downward spiral of my life. I could return to my initial response to MS, stay in bed and let the MS take from me everything I once knew. The struggle exhausted me, and sometimes all the effort made no difference.

One morning my doctor came in to check me. I asked, "Will I ever walk again?"

"Roxanne, for as long as I have known you, I have known you to be a fighter. Yes, I have no doubt that you will walk again."

With his faith in me, I grew so determined that after three physical therapy sessions, I struggled up from my wheelchair and grabbed the railing on the wall. *Baby steps, Roxanne.* With one hand on that and the other on the wheelchair, I "wall walked" all around the corridors. My doctor's words rang in my head and drove me to walk those corridors until I thought I would wear a path in the floor.

I discovered a person could do things others said were impossible. And I determined to be such a person.

Yet as hard as I tried, I couldn't shake the depression and the slow death sentence that hung over me.

It took years for doctors to find the right medications and dosages to combat the depression, relentless pain, and spasms MS dished out daily. Even with a new house, and despite my fighting nature, the pain and depression were too much, and the suicidal thoughts returned.

Finally the dark side won.

On a cold, crisp day I went for a walk with a bag of unused medications and a bottle of water. My lovable dog Stripe, a boxer, pranced beside me as I went to the farthest point on our property. I sat on a boulder under an apple tree and stayed there a long time. She lay quietly beside me.

I can't take it anymore. I looked at the bag.

With each exhale my breath lingered in the air like a shroud.

I looked up. Along our property line old fence posts leaned into the ground. The very ones Uncle Paul had set years ago. I pictured him tirelessly digging and setting them until the end of the day. I could see myself watching him work, swishing my hands in the tall grass and getting any tool he asked for.

Uncle Paul would be so disappointed in me for giving up and not being the fighter he had told me I was. Tears streamed down my face. *How can I do this to my family?* But I was drowning in despair, overwhelmed with visions of a deteriorating future.

Hands shaking, I opened the bag and picked up the first bottle of pills.

Stripe nudged me.

I reviewed my plan one more time. *Am I ready to do this?*

She nudged me again, in the direction of the house.

Will God have mercy on me?

The dog pawed me and prodded me.

Stop it! I didn't say.

Then I was the one who stopped.

Stripe kept nudging.

Why are you acting this way?

The bag felt suddenly menacing, and I didn't need an answer.

I got off that rock and headed home. The dog saved my life that day.

When David learned about this he called the doctor, and I stayed in the psych ward for two weeks.

Months after that my neurologist asked me about my depression. I told him I thought about sitting in the closed garage, turning on the car, and dying of carbon monoxide poisoning. That landed me in the psych ward again. Note to self: Beware of telling your doctor you are having suicidal thoughts.

To slap my senses back into place, I wanted a reminder of my selfish and repeated efforts to end my life with pills. So I had David drag that boulder, where Stripe and I had gone, from the back of the property and set it in the retaining wall of our front yard. We call it "Suicide Rock."

David grew exhausted with my endless volley of being a fighter one day and suicidal the next. Finally he sat me down, looked intensely into my eyes, and said, "Roxie, you have a choice to make. What are you going to do? Are you going to give in to MS and be miserable the rest of your life? Or are you going to turn this around the way you've turned everything else around?"

His words seized me. As if putting me under arrest, they pinned me down, handcuffed me, and forced me to face the facts I'd avoided: I was causing him grief he could no longer bear, betraying my faith in God, and living a big contradiction between strength and weakness.

He went on, "Are you going to fight back? Are you going to be thankful for the days God is giving you? And are you going to be thankful for the things you can still do? What choice will you make?"

Those questions were like keys that freed me from the handcuffs. They woke me up. I had been letting this disease take charge of my life, but it didn't have to be that way. My husband led me in the decision that turned my life around.

The turn took months of struggle between failure and success. I knew I had to trust God for the same good things that had happened when I trusted Him in the past. But I was scared and harbored nagging doubts. If I put myself completely in God's hands, would He really catch me every time I fell? Or would He let me become paralyzed and slide into an agonizing death?

God seemed to give me a clear indication He would now carry me because even though I could no longer work, our finances held up. We kept the house, paid medical bills, and had food on the table.

Step by step I put myself more in God's hands. I didn't completely get there, but I was more in than out. I still harbored doubts, but my faith grew bigger. I still battled depression, but my fighting spirit grew stronger.

I deliberately chose to enjoy every single day I was alive and strive to get my life back. Some days the discomfort would be too much to take, but I determined to cope and persevere.

Among the biggest trials to endure was a year-long round of chemotherapy treatments. My doctor did this in effort to force the MS into remission. Every three weeks I had dark blue poison intravenously pumped into me. Besides getting sick every time, something worse—no, better—happened. My already-thin hair completely fell out. And my dear husband shaved the leftover fuzzy clumps.

Most women grieve over their loss of hair after chemotherapy. And until now I would have wailed. But I was oddly relieved. Most of my adult life I had to endure embarrassing comments and explain why my hair was so thin. But now I finally had a good reason. And I even got sympathy from friends and strangers alike.

As I overcame my hardships, good things started happening.

When I first got diagnosed, David and I were both in a large symphonic band. He played trumpet and I played clarinet. I had once been a good player but was reduced to a beginner's level because my left hand went totally numb, my vision blurred, and I could not comprehend the music. I felt dejected and decided to never play again. David had other plans. He now bought me a $3,000 professional clarinet, which we could not afford. After returning it three times because it didn't have the right sound, we were able to contact the man who designed it, and he personally picked one with perfect pitch.

But I couldn't feel my fingers on my left hand, so how would I know if they were seated correctly over the keys? It was impossible. But David insisted. I didn't know how I could play without feeling my left fingers, but somehow—with God's help and practicing three times harder than I would have if I were normal—I did it. My comprehension was a problem, but despite many mistakes I would not give up. To this day I play with David in the Richfield Church of the Nazarene's band ensemble, and as I do I can still see in his eyes the boy I met in seventh-grade band—the boy my mother said God had made just for me.

An elderly couple in my church were my parents' best friends and were like parents to me. I casually mentioned that I loved music and thought it would be wonderful if our church had a hand-bell choir. A few months later that couple purchased three octaves of hand bells and two octaves of hand chimes. I formed a bell choir, which was the first thing since my diagnosis that made me feel I had purpose in life. For thirteen years I directed that group.

I had never acted before, but I studied at our local theater in downtown Lapeer. One day I landed the lead female role of Ethel Thayer in the play *On Golden Pond*. I memorized 63 pages of script—I don't know how, but I did. I performed perfectly through five shows. It was one thing on my bucket list I never thought I'd do.

I had always wanted to quilt. So my girl friend taught me, despite the numb fingers on my left hand that I often pierced. I started drawing and painting again. I planted a perennial garden. I cared for the elderly in our church, particularly the couple who purchased the hand bells. I've cared for many elderly in our church over the past eighteen years. And I taught our church's young people every Wednesday evening in the "Twenty-Something" group.

And during these later years, God did something else far beyond my expectations.

Mom developed Alzheimer's and went into a nursing home, so Dad spent his last four years alone. He couldn't totally care for himself. He had never written a check in his life and didn't know junk mail from a bill. My brother couldn't help Dad at that time, which meant I had to start caring for him. I was angry. Why should I help that tormentor? He deserved to go to hell. I was even nervous to be alone with him.

Very grudgingly, I went to help him at my childhood prison—I mean home. Every day.

My therapist always wanted me to call my father out on the issues, but I could never bring myself to do that. I also knew he would deny everything, because he thought we'd lived the perfect life of Norman Rockwell paintings.

As I did chores for him, God began speaking to me. Day after day, I sensed the Holy Spirit's prompting that I should put the past behind me and forgive that man.

You have got to be kidding.

No way was I going to do that. It was hard just being around him.

But as I helped him, I began to feel pity. I could see the sadness in his eyes, and his demeanor gradually softened. Seeing Dad so helpless without Mom began to soften me as well. As I cleaned rotting food from the refrigerator and clutter all around the house, I perceived that this was *not* the spic-and-span father I had known all my life. This was a man who had given up, much like I once did. I soon learned that he missed Mom and nothing mattered to him anymore. I felt so sad.

Imagine that. I actually cared. I knew touching and moving Dad's things could be tricky, but I asked him if I could change the house to make it safer for him. That was the beginning of my new journey with Dad. It took me four years to completely clean the house, the attic, and the dreaded basement, with my brother's help in tackling those spider condominiums. The garage became my brother's and David's domain. *Dad's* garage was a *guy* area—not a place for women. So much the better!

I can't remember exactly when or how I did it, but I forgave him. It happened while God performed a miracle in me. By my serving Dad, God, in His amazing grace, healed me of my emotional pain and enabled me to let go of my hatred.

I saw how both Dad and I resulted from circumstances beyond our control. As he was a product of his mother's cruelty, I clearly saw how I became a product of his. He had to have carried a terrible burden for the father and husband he'd been.

Then Dad became a Christian.

No way.

He was still ornery, but yes, he did.

He didn't like church, but he watched evangelical TV shows and read his Bible daily. His eyes were opened about his past behavior. He never could speak about it, but his actions spoke loudly. I could tell he felt guilty over the way he had treated Mom during their married life. Every day he went to the nursing home and spent several hours with her. He also felt remorse for the way he had treated me.

Added to that, the loneliness caused Dad to become severely depressed to where he didn't want to live anymore. We countered that by packing a lifetime's worth of a loving father-and-daughter relationship into four precious years. We were no longer enemies but two people who enjoyed each other's company so much that my childhood of tears was washed away.

Dad made me promise that if he died before Mom, I would look after her as he had finally done, visiting every day. Of course I would honor that promise. We both loved Mom with all our hearts.

On Easter Sunday 2003, Dad passed away. We found him cold and stiff in his favorite chair. I screamed hysterically and begged him to wake up. I had hated this man most of my life, but here I was inconsolable, pleading with him to come back to me, because we had so many more things to do together. After his body was taken away, I curled up on his bed for two hours.

He died with the telephone in his hand, which meant it happened the night before, right after I said, "I love you, Dad. I'll see you tomorrow."

He said, "Thank you." Then pressed the off button and died peacefully, the way he had hoped.

If Mom had not gone into the nursing home, Dad and I would never have mended our relationship, and he would have died with my dancing on his grave. I now felt ashamed for even thinking such a thing. If he had died with my still hating him, I might never have recovered from the burden of guilt.

God worked all these things out and miraculously transformed my emotions. He gave both my father and me a new heart.

I grieved losing him just as we were growing close and correcting our dysfunctional relationship. Many people have circumstances similar to mine, but they may feel out of control, and perhaps for a while they are. But from my experience, I can see how, and why, each difficulty can lead us to turn a wrong into a right *if* we soften our hearts and look closely at the *whys* in each situation.

Though the onset of multiple sclerosis thrust David and me on a daunting path, not once did David feel sorry for himself because of me. He has always been by my side, crying with me, encouraging me, and telling me not to give in. He holds me in his arms and prays for me every day, asking God to give me a "good" day. If not for him I would have lain down and let MS rampage over me. But David's encouraging words, pure love, and devotion have buoyed me through countless hard times. My tears flow as I say this. Because of David I have chosen to fight—and do things that seem impossible.

The most impossible was about to happen.

Chapter 6

DISEMBODIED

I know a man in Christ who fourteen years ago was caught up to the third heaven. Whether it was in the body or out of the body I do not know—God knows. And I know that this man—whether in the body or apart from the body I do not know, but God knows—was caught up to paradise (2 Corinthians 12:2–4).

How suddenly we breach the partition between this dimension and the next.

On a warm and sunny Wednesday in May 2006, flowers were in bloom, the sky was deep blue, and the grass a lush green. That evening I smiled as I drove home from teaching my church's Twenty-Something group. I was so happy as I was driving my bright yellow Mini Cooper with windows down, Christian music blasting on the radio, the sweet smell of first cut grass, and the wind in my face. My vanity license plate read "roxin8r." *Look out, here I come!*

This particular evening's lesson had been on the subject "Why do bad things happen to good people?" They were so interested, and I had so much to tell. We talked for two hours. One guy's grandmother had chronic illnesses and was dying. Another wanted to know why she couldn't find a job and had to endure so much difficulty as a result. One more wanted to know why her mother had early-onset Alzheimer's. Each one had a why-do-bad-things-happen-to-good-people story.

I was excited to tell David how engaging the class had been, so I went to the barn where he was restoring a wooden canoe. As I gushed about the great evening, my head felt woozy, and my body grew fatigued. I've called this "hitting the wall." It comes with no reason or warning.

He led me inside and put me to bed as the dizziness and weakness became almost unbearable.

Thursday morning came with no relief, the kind of day we often referred to as "just one of those days," where I would weather out the storm in bed for as long as it took.

Friday morning launched me into the most painful muscle spasms I had encountered since being diagnosed with multiple sclerosis twelve years earlier.

Saturday got still worse. My muscles ached from the contorting spasms, as if I'd done a triathlon. And the dizziness was so overwhelming that I could not figure out if I was right side up, down, sideways, spinning, or lying down. It was like being on an insane roller coaster, as if the G-forces pulled me to the left, the right, up, down, and sideways. I felt continuously sick, and my headache felt like a perpetual explosion. I could no longer tolerate any kind of sound or sight, which only amplified the pain. My condition deteriorated to where my body simply could not cope, and I began to slip in and out of consciousness.

David's sister Becky, a nurse practitioner, stopped by to check on me. As I drifted in and out, Becky tried to talk me into going to the hospital.

"What's the point? It's not worth it. I give up. Just leave me alone."

David wanted to call my doctor. I had made David promise never to take me to the hospital again. I had been admitted to

Crittenton Hospital in Rochester Hills, Michigan, so many times by now, I began to refer to it as my "vacation spot." Only two months earlier I had basked in a steel-framed bed under their fluorescent lights. I did *not* want to go back. I begged David not to call, because I knew the doctor would want me admitted again.

I was tired of suffering and complaining to my family and of feeling like a continual burden. My future promised little more than agonizing deterioration, and now seemed a good time to let my life end before it got worse. I just wanted everyone to let me be and let me die.

Then it was lights out for me again as I lost consciousness.

Lying flat in bed, I suddenly glimpsed Dad and Uncle Paul coming toward me. Dad had died three years earlier and Uncle Paul a year after that. I was so excited to see them again that I sat straight up in bed and called out their names with laughter. As soon as I did that they disappeared. Disappointment flooded me. I felt I needed them. Had I frightened them away? Why would they leave me?

David heard me call to them and said, "That's it. She's going to the hospital."

My eyes closed and stayed that way. I couldn't move or speak, but I felt David and my daughter Sara dressing me. Then a car ride. My body jarred with every bump and turn in the road. David's hand reached over my nose and mouth—I was still breathing. He sounded so scared. "Just stay with me, sweetie. It'll all be okay. You'll come out of this, you always do. It will be okay... It will be okay."

But I don't want it to be okay! Don't you understand?

At the hospital the emergency team surrounded me in nonstop commotion. People tugged at me, yelled out orders, and cut off my clothing. One of them called out, "Her body is so cold. We can't get blood or start an IV." *What is going on?* I felt so warm and comfortable. I heard them talking about putting tubes down my nose, taking arterial blood gasses, and trying numerous locations for blood samples and IV lines. "Finally," I heard one say, "I got an IV."

Another said, "Got a blood sample from her foot." *Her foot?* Since when did they start taking blood from someone's foot? This sounded serious.

While David was apparently parking the car, they asked where "the husband" was. They sounded sarcastic, as if David had done something to harm me. When he came in, they interrogated him about what may have caused this unconsciousness. "Did she try to commit suicide?" "How long has she had MS?" "Did she have a seizure?" "Has she been sick?"

Yes I've been sick! I have chronic progressive multiple sclerosis, not hay fever.

Everyone seemed frantic but me. I was comfortable, warm, at peace, and in complete relaxation. I was pain free. I felt totally protected and safe from whatever was going on with my body—except for the emergency team trying to wake me up. As hard as they tried, they couldn't do it. Over and over they ground their fists into my chest and raised my arm over my head, letting it drop onto my face—techniques used to cause pain and wake an unconscious person.

Oh, that irritated me. Every time they lifted my arm and dropped it, I bopped myself in my own face. Come on, if I were conscious, would I be stupid enough to let my arm smack into my face twenty times? *Good grief! Stop doing that,* I screamed in my mind but couldn't say. I felt no pain but kept thinking they would eventually break my nose. I could hear the doctors whispering something. *What are they saying?* I felt so helpless. *Why can't I just wake up?* I could tell them I was fine and this would all be over. I could go home. I was angry that David had gone against my wishes and brought me to the hospital in the first place.

As time passed in the emergency room, I sensed myself floating. I rose straight above my bed, and suddenly I was able to look down and see myself lying helpless. I looked down at everyone in the room. I saw all the technicians and doctors working on me. I saw my body between them all. A technician did an EKG on me. He was gentle and quiet, but I could sense his uneasiness as he lowered my gown so he could place the lead wires on my chest. When he finished, he neglected to raise my gown. I was so embarrassed. *Cover me up!* I tried to yell without a voice, without a body. I could only look down at myself as if I were another person. Finally David was allowed in, and he immediately covered me—the one I was looking down on.

I could not figure out how I was floating without anything holding me up. My senses told me my arms and legs were somehow being held in suspension by a rope or a belt. But they weren't. How could this be? I had never heard of such a thing. How could I hear and understand what was happening to me, yet be totally comfortable, feel such peace, and be floating in the air?

I heard David say he was leaving for a while to make some calls. He obviously needed support for what was coming and thought for sure I was going to die. While he called, they took my body out of ER to do a CAT scan.

I felt giddy as I floated above myself, whizzing through hallways, looking down at my comatose body. Amusement parks have nothing on floating above yourself and getting a free ride through midair.

I also had the ability to look at my surroundings. Doors everywhere. Though I'd once worked in a hospital, I suppose I noticed this now because it was the first time I'd passed through them from this height. I was curious to know what each room was for. Let's see…one said x-ray, another had the radiation symbol, others were unmarked. I felt as I were sightseeing at tourist attractions.

The hallway was lined with empty gurneys; my own dodged them as we passed. Like bumper cars with a driver who managed not to bump. This was fun!

But the medical personnel were all quite somber. They were dressed in blue scrubs and looked important, and each one seemed to have a critical task. *How very serious*, I thought.

While I got the scans, David and I were separated for the first time since coming to the hospital. *Was he all right?* The pace now slowed because most of the tests and procedures were completed. The sense of urgency was lowering. Then they rolled me back to the emergency room. Someone commented that I had been there for eight hours.

I heard them talking about moving me to the hospice ward. *Isn't that a place to die?* Then I heard David's voice telling me once again that everything would be all right. He said, "Honey, we will get you better. I promise." He asked one of the nurses if I was going to die. She quieted him, telling him that I may be able to hear. She knew!

Then he cried. I watched him hold my limp hand and sob.

I don't know how, but though I was separate from my body, I wasn't like a detached or indifferent ghost. I could feel emotion. My heart was breaking for my dear husband. I grieved over the pain I was causing him.

Then things got even stranger. My physical body below responded to the wrenching emotion in my separated, suspended self. The bond of love between David and me had by now grown so powerful that I could feel his pain as I always did. And tears welled up in the eyes of my body on the bed. Through all the invasive procedures the staff had done on me, I had felt no pain. But with my husband's tears, I did. Tears trickled down. I watched him take a handkerchief from his pocket and wipe them away. *David, I'm shedding these tears for you. Don't you know I can hear you? I'm here with you. Can't you feel my emotions the way I feel yours?* I thought the tears would let David know I could hear him. Yet he later told me that he was unaware I could hear anything at all. Sometimes guys just don't get it!

I tried as hard as I could to move just one finger to comfort and let him know that I had heard him, but I couldn't. My body on the bed was paralyzed. Yet it shed tears out of the emotion in my disembodied self. I do not understand that.

One by one the people David had called came in, and I watched and heard each one from my aerial point of view. Most of them spoke directly to me. Bev said, "Come back! I need you to continue directing the bell choir." Krystal pleaded that she loved me and needed me in her life. Pastor Drew prayed for me and tried to comfort David. David's sister Becky helped the nurses and prayed for me with her husband, John.

My father-in-law, Dad Wermuth, said a prayer, then looked at me and said, "She looks so peaceful, just like she is sleeping." He whispered in my ear, "I love you." I could not respond to him in our usual comical way by saying "thank you" instead of "I love you too." My heart was breaking because I wanted to thank everyone for loving me so much and driving all the way down there to be with David and me. But I could not.

All the tests were run and final words said. Nothing else to do, and a growing sadness filled the air. The staff asked our friends and family to leave. Only Becky and John remained. The staff told them they thought I was in end-stage MS. I was a goner. With death imminent, I had no place to go but the hospice ward.

They wheeled me out, and I floated above my body the whole way. Unlike the first ride, I no longer felt that amusement-park giddiness. I grew somber—but not for myself. I grieved for my family who thought I was about to die. If only I could tell them, somehow, that I was all right. I felt no pain. And I was at total peace, except for hurting for them.

I tried as hard as I could to put mind over matter—unusual because they were separate—and make myself wake up, but I just couldn't.

I was put in a private room, where family could be alone with their loved one who was dying.

The hospice nurse was so kind. She said, "Honey, you'll be all right. We're going to take good care of you." She talked to me as if I were still there, still alive. She was so gentle, and her sweet nature touched me deeply, even though I was still split between the bed and the ceiling.

Becky and David disagreed with my being moved here and went out of my room to insist that the staff call my doctor, who had treated me since my initial diagnosis and knew I was a fighter. I saw that Becky was too. She *screamed* at the nurses, demanding that they call my doctor. I loved her spunk.

Something unusual happened to me while they were out of the room. Although no one else was there, I didn't feel alone. Someone seemed to be with me, an older woman. *Who is that? Someone I know? Am I imagining this?* I never knew what happened or who this may, or may not, have been. I cannot explain this.

"Take her to ICU," I heard. In came an orderly and rolled me out. *Oh no. I'm being moved again? I like it here with this nice nurse. She's the only one who's treated me as if I'm still here.* She even looked sweet, a little older than the others, short and a bit chubby. In that brief time, I had grown fond of her, and she had become my friend. Now I was being taken from her.

As I went, the staff encouraged my family and friends to go home and get some rest.

Everything in ICU seemed stark and white. Cold, not cozy like the hospice room had been. My body lay below me, surrounded by machines, monitors, wires, tubes, beeping sounds, and blinking lights. John appeared and gently stroked my head as he prayed. Becky came in with a nurse and made sure my doctor's orders were *completely* understood. Her forceful instructions made me happy. *Go Becky!* I couldn't say. Then John and Becky left, and I was completely alone.

Three nurses came in, checked my vitals, and began to talk about me. One said, "I guess she tried to commit suicide but didn't take enough pills."

Another said, "Maybe one more would have done it." They all giggled and left.

Later estimates would indicate that by now I had been floating above my body for almost twelve hours.

Suddenly, I felt my disembodied self rise higher. *What's going on?* Bright lights dimmed. Voices, phones, and beeping monitors fell silent. I gradually rose higher. Past the fluorescent lights. Through the ceiling. Upward. I could no longer see myself below, and everything faded. All this time I felt warm and peaceful. I had no idea what was happening or where I was going, I only sensed it would be very good.

This change happened only after family, friends, and nurses left. It was as if the absence of people who loved and prayed for me, or were supposed to care for me, released me to move on. It's a mystery, but I cannot think of any other reason why I didn't float upward sooner—or why I didn't continue floating in the same way I'd been doing for so long.

Where was I going? I was no longer in the hospital. Or on earth. I was in a new dimension. I don't know how I got there, but I ended up in a tunnel, a long dark tunnel that seemed to have no beginning or end.

Chapter 7

GOD'S WAITING ROOM

In my Father's house are many rooms; if it were not so, I would have told you. I am going there to prepare a place for you (John 14:2).

I found myself alone in a warm, dark, seemingly endless tunnel. It was completely quiet, no beeping of monitors or footsteps of nurses.

Where am I? I lay on my back, suspended, just floating. I turned my head in all directions to get an idea of this place. It was round, approximately eight to ten feet in diameter. Previously I had never heard any near-death-going-to-heaven stories, so I was mystified at what was happening to me. I knew I had left ICU and floated up. Apparently a new journey was about to begin.

Somehow I knew not to be afraid, that something wonderful would happen.

The sides of the tunnel looked as if they were made of curved, smooth tiles, colored richly in a deep earth tone. At first, I thought they were glistening with water. I soon realized they shimmered with what appeared to be gold and diamonds that lit the tunnel just enough for me to see the outlines of each tile. *This is so beautiful!*

I floated motionless in total peace for what seemed like a very long time. There seemed to be no gravity. And I wondered how I could be suspended this way, much as I had been in the hospital. This was more like floating peacefully in a calm ocean, yet there was no water. I didn't care if I had an answer; I simply didn't want it to end.

I was so content I could have spent the rest of my life in there. My body felt no pain or discomfort. I was not depressed, nor did I have any negative thoughts. I felt comfortable, protected, and safe. The temperature felt perfect. The sense of peace completely saturated me. I struggle to find the human vocabulary to accurately describe the experience. Strange as it seems, I was happier than I had ever been in my life—and I was in a darkened tunnel!

Whether I was able to remember my earthly life and MS or not, I don't know. Either way I thought of nothing I left behind. I was completely absorbed in comfort, rest, and serenity. I didn't know what this tunnel was about. Or why I was there. Or where it would take me. I only felt that it was good.

While floating motionless for so long, I became aware of two figures approaching me, visible between my feet. Though they were far away, a dim light behind them made their outlines visible.

Very slowly they glided toward me, as though they too were floating. I still felt no fear. Somehow I knew this would also be a good thing—an awesome event. Who were these two people, and what did they want of me?

As they got nearer, they came into focus, and in the faint glimmer of the tunnel walls, I could tell exactly who they were. My father and Uncle Paul—the same two who had appeared to me before I went into the hospital. I thought I'd never see them again, yet here they were! Though I was never lonely in the tunnel, I was still overjoyed to see them return.

Then I found myself rotating upright to my feet until I looked at them face to face. They were both so young and vibrant, restored to their youth and perfect health. Then they smiled. And from inside them, shining through their mouths, radiated bright light. I had never seen anyone smile like this, never seen such a glow, especially striking in the tunnel's dimness. They both seemed to have an abundance of joy and peace I have never witnessed before. Except for their identities, nothing about them was earthly.

Without their speaking a word to me, I somehow knew they had come to meet me and maybe keep me company in the tunnel. They seemed as happy to see me as I was to see them. I felt a warm love connecting their hearts to mine, with a sense of belonging, as if we somehow became as one. Then I intuitively knew they wanted me to follow them. They turned and began gliding in the direction from which they had come. And I glided along behind them.

The dim light remained in the distance. And the farther we went, the brighter the light grew. Then I saw that the tunnel did have an end. As we neared it, the light grew more brilliant, like the sun, yet beyond human description.

As I stood at the tunnel's edge, Dad and Uncle Paul stepped out. They stopped in a meadow and turned to me, beckoning with outstretched arms.

Until now I had no earthly thoughts. Suddenly I hesitated as one entered my mind. *This bright light is going to hurt my eyes because I was in the dark tunnel so long.* Then another thought came. *I'm barefoot, and the meadow will prick my feet, which are hypersensitive.*

Dad and Uncle Paul continued to beckon me.

Certainly I could trust them. But one more earthly thought stopped me. I knew I was stepping out on holy ground, or holy something. I felt totally unworthy, stained with my past sins.

Yet they continued to beckon me with their outstretched arms. I stepped out.

It was like stepping into the sun. But there was no single source. Light shone from everywhere around. Yet it didn't hurt my eyes at all. Oddly, I felt no warm or cool sensation, only a sense of perfect comfort. All around was what seemed like an endless blue sky. I stood awestruck.

To my surprise, the surface below me was firm but unbelievably soft, caressing my feet as if I were walking on thick cotton balls.

Then Dad and Uncle Paul embraced me as if welcoming me to a long-overdue family reunion. I felt I had reached my final destination, my ultimate home.

Words were not necessary. We communicated every idea and feeling through a kind of heavenly telepathy that flowed freely between all three of us.

Yet it didn't seem like just us. I sensed we were surrounded by countless others. Though I could not see them, the welcome seemed to come from millions, even billions, of souls who were there, beyond us, all around, celebrating and welcoming me.

A deep sense of belonging cradled me and wrapped me in a feeling of never-ending love, comfort, and safety. This feeling was softer than a down blanket caressing my skin. Although I sensed no atmospheric temperature or conditions, it was like being wrapped in a warm blanket in the cold of winter. The air—if I can call it that—seemed to cuddle me in velvet and envelop me in this wondrous softness. And there was a connectedness to it, as though I had been knit into my surroundings—like a whole new level of being one with Christ. I now have a richer grasp of those words.

We stood in front of the most breathtaking sight I had ever seen—a vast meadow carpeted with millions and millions of bright yellow flowers, beyond what my eyes could see. Astonishingly, I could distinguish the minute details of every single flower. They each had five soft petals, and the whole flower was the size of a nickel. All around hovered a bright blue sky and the brilliant light. No color pallet on earth could match these vivid colors.

Then three of us ran—effortlessly—through this bright yellow meadow that stretched endlessly. I was able to run like the wind! Across hills and valleys, we dashed in every direction with no limit of strength and no limit of flowers. We never grew tired or short of breath, and we never fell down.

As I ran I felt something bouncing on my shoulders.

Hair.

Thick locks of it, long and flowing in the air, bobbed up and down. That alone made me burst with joy. My wishes and prayers since childhood finally came true.

We laughed together, and I felt overwhelming peace and joy. I was amazed at the intense feeling of love I had for both of them. I had adored Uncle Paul my entire life, yet hated my father most of my life. I now loved both men equally. This overwhelming love was so great, so intense, and beyond my comprehension.

At the same time I felt humbled. How could someone like me, stained by my past, step—or run—on holy ground? God had forgiven my sins, though I had not forgiven myself. Yet here I was.

All this time I was deliriously happy. No room in my mind for anything else besides pure joy. I was an adult but felt like a child, experiencing everything through the awe of a child's eyes. And it was all without limit.

While I was in the meadow, my entire being became one with God in His Light. A heightened sensitivity and a clear awareness came over me. Yet I was too ecstatic and overwhelmed to rationally process the experience at the time. After my return to earth, I gradually made sense of it. I also learned I had been in a state of unconsciousness for nearly 24 hours. Putting together the reports of hospital activity surrounding me, I found that the first twelve hours

I floated above my body and the second twelve I spent in the tunnel and the meadow. Though it would take months before I could fully understand everything that happened to me in those 24 hours, in due time all would be revealed—and would transform many parts of my life.

To carry that retrospective understanding into the immediate heavenly experience, I will try to express those aspects of life in heaven that were revealed to me.

From the instant my toes touched that soft ground, everything in me completely changed. Previously I never thought I was worthy of entering heaven. But not once did I think of my past sins or unworthiness. And as imperfect as I was—and am—not once did I think I hadn't earned the right to be in heaven. Being there is not about rights or even earning anything. We get there because we repent and give ourselves to this God who infinitely loves us despite ourselves. His intent is that we experience the perfection He has waiting for us.

I became weightless compared to the heaviness of guilt I once carried. I truly felt like a butterfly, fluttering effortlessly and beautifully through the bright yellow flowers of that endless heavenly field.

The dazzling light was more than just light. It must have been from God, because it felt like a bath that washed my inner darkness away and made me clean. I had known the Bible's teaching on forgiveness, yet I often doubted God would actually forgive a sinner like me. Being raised in the church, I heard a lot about being "saved and sanctified," that is, getting right with God and living a holy life. I theoretically believed it. But a part of me always remained saturated with guilt that would not come out and darkness that would not leave.

I felt I was bathing in a shower of God's purifying light, of His presence, that washed all the gunk out of my being. I knew I was God's child, and I knew He loved me. My doubts disappeared under this cascade of unconditional love. I felt—and indeed I was—totally purified, inside and out. I concluded that Jesus really did pay the penalty for my sin, and He really did forgive me completely. There's no other clean like that.

As I ran under that shower of light, overwhelmed in cleansing love, I thought my heart would burst. I sensed that even if I did burst, I would become one with everything around me because the whole place felt saturated in love without measure. This realization/ awareness was instilled as the light bathed me. The love is all equal. Intense. Enormous—full of purity, peace, happiness, joy, comfort, laughter, contentment, and perfection.

This love will fill our entire beings.

There is no difference between the love of a father versus that of a mother, a first spouse or a second spouse, boyfriend, girlfriend, a child, or any other relationship. The love is so immense that there is no distinction between people. It is the purest form of love one could imagine. Even then it's beyond our grasp.

Soon after I returned from God's Waiting Room, David asked, "So what happens if a spouse dies, gets remarried, and all three are in heaven together?" He didn't realize that all the love is equal. There are no jealousies because we are all one. We are like brothers and sisters, just as Jesus said in answer to a similar question about a woman who had seven successive husbands, each of whom died: "'At the resurrection, whose wife will she be of the seven, since all of them were married to her?' Jesus responded, 'At the resurrection people will neither marry nor be given in marriage; they will be like the angels in heaven'" (Matthew 22:28, 30).

I absorbed so much awareness of heaven during the hours I spent there. But they felt like moments. It's not the way we feel on earth that "time flies." It's way beyond that. I experienced a clear explanation for this: heaven has no measure of time. There are no minutes, hours, days, weeks, months, or years. There are no clocks. The Bible expresses it this way: "With the Lord a day is like a thousand years, and a thousand years are like a day" (2 Peter 3:8).

How can I explain this? It just is. It's a perfect heavenly dimension we will enter when our earthly lives end. It is a never-ending resource of incredible love, peace, and blissfulness that has no end.

I perceived that the word "forever" does not exist, or has no meaning, because it's a measure of time. Forever has a beginning but no end. Yet in heaven I sensed we will not realize when the beginning is because heaven has no beginning or end. And although we call heaven our eternal home, "eternal" itself is a reference of time. The reality exists beyond that.

The whole time I never had a negative thought. I focused only on heaven itself. It may be that our minds will be erased of all negative thoughts when we get to heaven. We will no longer have the pain of regrets that have followed us throughout our lives. Bad memories faded and went away. And we will not be occupied with worries about anything on earth. For the first time in my entire life, my mind was clear of all negative thoughts, pain, and worries. We will be washed, as I was, in God's light. We will be purified through Him and there will be no pain or suffering of any kind, emotional or physical. I was in pure bliss. If that were the only event that happened to me, it would have been enough by itself.

Sometimes I tell people, "Think about the happiest time of your entire life—think hard—now multiply that by a million and you might be halfway there." There was no opportunity, or at least no need, to think of the past. It was irrelevant.

As I reveled in my new existence (and my long, thick hair) it never occurred to me how I died or got there. I only knew I was there.

I perceive that when we are on this other side, we will not remember how we died. During my time in the tunnel and the heavenly meadow, my mind was continuously clear. But I had no thoughts of my horrible condition before going into the coma, or how desperately I wanted to die, or what went on in ER as I saw and heard everything for twelve hours. None. And immediately before I entered this other dimension, I was near death. All of that was erased.

The whole time I was in heaven I had no thoughts of earth. I cannot say with authority whether or not we will remember our lives on earth, but my experience suggests that we may not think of it at all. I saw this in at least four ways.

One is that we will apparently not remember our earthly sufferings. Or even if we do, they would have no effect on us. While I was in the tunnel, I was aware of how much better I felt than I had previously. And before stepping out I expected my feet to be supersensitive, an effect of MS, and thus feel painfully pricked by the meadow. But once I stepped out, those kinds of thoughts vanished. All that "time" I had no thoughts of the hospital, the coma, suffering, or anything related to my illness. Whether I was capable of remembering my earthly suffering or not, I do not know. I can only know that I didn't. My mind had no room for anything but the splendor of heaven. Walking and running barefoot felt natural, and I reveled in that. Similarly, the Bible says of the new heaven and new earth that God "will wipe every tear from their eyes. There will be no more death or mourning or crying or pain, for the old order of things has passed away" (Revelation 21:4).

Another is that our earthly status has nothing to do with our identity in heaven. There are no classes of people that have anything to do with who we were or what we had on earth. Those who enter this paradise will do so equally by responding to Jesus Christ. (I don't mean to get too religious here, but the Jesus thing seems to be the key factor—and it's not about being religious but about connecting with God while we're still on earth. We can't earn this eternal life; we can only receive it. Being a good person doesn't cut it because we could never be good enough for a perfect God.) We won't run in the rat race of jobs and accomplishments. And we will not take to heaven anything we own on earth. Those things are just that—things. Nothing earthly has any place in heaven. The word *things* and all it implies is utterly insignificant from heaven's point of view, where possessions and accomplishments are not important enough to even enter our minds. Heaven will instead be full of the beauty and splendor of what God has stored up for us. While the Bible indicates that some will be rewarded for their obedience and sacrifice—like Jesus' "great is your reward" statements in Matthew 5:12 and Luke 6:23 and 35—it also indicates that earthly accomplishments and possessions have no place in heaven, even to the point of saying, "What is highly valued among men is detestable in God's sight" (Luke 16:15). A heavy statement, but it appears to be true.

A third is that we will have limited awareness of those we know who are still on earth. The whole time I was in the heavenly meadow, I had no remembrance of anyone on earth. Not even my family. Whether I was prevented from remembering, incapable of remembering, or just overwhelmed with all the glory, I am not sure. So I'm not saying we absolutely cannot have any memory of them, but I was in such a state of bliss that I had no space in my consciousness to think of anything I'd left behind. The thought of David, the girls, my friends, and my family—and of leaving them—never entered my mind.

The last point here is similar but goes further. If we have friends or loved ones who died without a relationship with God, we will not remember them. This sounds harsh, and seems to write off people who aren't Christian enough, which is why I could not speak about it for years. And I wondered about it myself. I came to understand it's because God our Father loves us so much and intends to provide us with the perfection of His eternal presence in which we have no emotional pain. If we did remember unsaved loved ones, we would grieve. And grieving does not happen in this state of perfect joy.

This awareness was perhaps the most important. We can die and go to the eternal beyond in the blink of an eye. Have we truly done our best to bring others to faith? God seems to want us to know that we will have no knowledge of nonbelievers once we pass into this other dimension. On earth the thought of not remembering a loved one is painful. Yet when we get to heaven, God will remove all loss and negative thoughts from our minds, for He loves us and wants us to experience His perfection only.

Like it or not, consider the prospect that our loved ones in heaven do not miss us. From what I could tell, they may not even think about us. That may not make us happy here and now, but remember that a believer's ultimate destination is in God's presence. And the perspective from that place is eternal and far more important than ours on earth. Earthly years of sadness may be like the blink of an eye in heaven, where there is no place for sadness.

Yet when we arrive in heaven, those already there are able to recognize us as though time or distance were never a factor. This phenomenon could be something like when we're away from a person for a long time and stop thinking about him or her. Then suddenly we meet. We recognize the face and begin to recall what had slipped from our mind. Those in heaven seem to know we're coming, as if they got an announcement and come out to greet us. With family reunions at the top of the agenda, everyone's in party mode.

We in turn will recognize them, even though they are restored to perfect health and have light beaming from inside them.

On this side of heaven, we need not be sad for loved ones who die if they are connected with God. They are in His house, a state of eternal youthfulness, vibrancy, and indescribable delight.

We have much to look forward to. When we are reunited, sadness will be erased and we will not remember the pain and the years we were separated from them on earth.

I wished I could have stayed, but God had another plan.

Chapter 8

COMING BACK

For to me, to live is Christ and to die is gain. If I am to go on living in the body, this will mean fruitful labor for me. Yet what shall I choose? I do not know! I am torn between the two: I desire to depart and be with Christ, which is better by far; but it is more necessary for you that I remain in the body (Philippians 1:21–22).

All this time in heaven neither Dad nor Uncle Paul said a single word to me. The communication had all been somehow by a heavenly telepathy.

Then Uncle Paul spoke. In the same booming voice he had on earth, he called me by the name he had always used for me. It struck me that even personality characteristics like voice and mannerisms can carry into heaven. He bellowed, "Well, Rox. It's time for you to go back."

Instantly I became aware of my life back on earth. And sometimes I wonder if he became earthly to me for a reason. Only then did I grasp that if I stayed, I would leave my loved ones behind. David would be so hurt if I didn't return to him. Yet heaven was so perfect I didn't want to go back. I now remembered I had MS before coming here. *Ugh! Let me keep the meadow.*

"No, Uncle Paul, I don't want to go back."

It was as if I became human again. Was my sudden recollection of life and people on earth because Uncle Paul's directive snapped me out of my ecstasy enough for me to think of them? Or did his words set me into a re-entry mode connected with earth? I do not know. It happened so inexplicably. I didn't want this to happen. *Stop! Let's go back to laughing, telepathy, and bounding through the meadow.*

Here in heaven I was completely healthy and feeling good for the first time in twelve years. I didn't want to stop running. I felt so much love; everything was perfect. Nothing on earth was worth leaving this place.

Like the little girl I had once been, running alongside him, I pleaded, "Please, Uncle Paul! Please let me stay here with you!"

His face was kind and understanding. But his intent was clear.

"Pleeeease!"

He gently smiled the way people do when they regretfully have to disappoint someone. He slowly shook his head. "You have more to do in your life."

Then my father spoke, using the name he had called me during his last four years, which was the closest he could come to saying my name, which he never did speak. "Sis, remember the promise you made to take care of your mother if I died before she did? You promised to take care of her."

I knew exactly what he meant. Mom was in a nursing home suffering from end-stage Alzheimer's, and I had gone there every day with Dad before he died. She still needed my care.

Against my wishes the three of us were somehow back at the tunnel entrance. One minute in a field of flowers, the next back at the tunnel. *Why? What did this mean?* I don't know how we got there. We just went there in an instant.

Again Dad spoke, "Remember your promise."

Then I was gone.

Everything went dark. *I must be inside the tunnel.* But I saw no glittering walls. Only darkness. It wasn't as if I clicked my heels together like Dorothy in the *Wizard of Oz* and said, "There's no place like home." Rather than floating peacefully on my back as I had at the beginning, I unwillingly sped through the darkness, as if plunging into an abyss.

My eyes began to open, and despite my promise, I prayed I'd still be in the heavenly meadow. *Please, God, don't send me back.* I desperately willed my heart to stop beating, but it wouldn't. I tried to stop breathing, but my lungs demanded otherwise.

Stuck in a body that stubbornly came to life.

My eyes opened again. They hurt from the glare of the fluorescent lights, and I looked away. Yet compared to the brightness of heaven's light, these lights were dim.

I never went back into the tunnel. I just disappeared from heaven's light and reappeared under ceiling fixtures.

Did I really come back? Or is this just a figment of my imagination? I looked around. Had I really left in the first place?

This room I now lay in was the dream. Even the white paint seemed numb. An IV line was stuck in my arm, an oxygen tube in my nose, and other tubes dangled around my body. Compared to where I'd just been, this was *not* life. I lingered in confusion. Soon a woman came in, frightening me because her features seemed distorted, as though she were a witch. My eyes struggled to re-focus in the harsh lighting.

"You're awake," she said in a cold monotone. "Do you know where you are?"

"A hospital?"

"Yes."

She must be a nurse. My mind and vision were still blurry.

"Do you know what day it is?"

"No."

"Do you know what year it is?"

"No."

"You've been here about twenty-four hours. How are you feeling?"

Confusion and dread, aching to return to paradise. I was back in my wrecked body, unfortunately conscious in this hospital bed, probably hair deprived again, and talking to a nurse.

She checked the monitors and my blood pressure, the heart leads on my chest and the pulse oximeter on my finger. All seemed fine. "Welcome back."

Back to what? To my existence on earth, locked in this tomb of a body, where every day was a struggle? I did *not* want a welcome back. My mind and vision cleared. Instead of the beauty of heaven, I was now surrounded by tubes and blinking lights on monitors. Serenity gave way to beeping, shuffling papers, and voices. Worse, I was alone. So alone. Disappointment assaulted me. My heart weighed heavy.

The pain started biting and chewing at me again—worse than before because of bruises on my chest. I begged God to take me back. Lift me out of this again. I wanted to return to God's perfect presence. No sickness, aches, or spasms. Energetic and happy, romping through flowers under dazzling light.

Wasn't I good enough to stay with God? Why would He send me back? What purpose would keep me here on earth? But I did make that promise.

"Did you try to commit suicide?"

"Huh?" I was seeing and thinking clearer now. "Absolutely not. I would never do that." Well, there were those times I did. But this was not one of them.

"Do you remember how you got here?"

"Yes. My husband brought me here." *Twenty-four hours?* "What happened to me?"

"You've been comatose."

Then I remembered. Doctors and nurses surrounding me, grinding their fists on my chest trying to wake me, and sticking tubes into me; my floating and seeing everything around me; going to hospice and back; David crying; people visiting; three nurses joking; rising; the tunnel.

Nurses joking that I hadn't overdosed enough to die. This nurse was one of them. "I saw you and heard what you said about me."

She peered over her clipboard, pen frozen in mid-report. "What do you mean?"

I told her. And let her shock set in.

"I want to call my husband." I struggled to get the number right, but my fingers refused to work, so she dutifully dialed the call.

"David, I'm back."

"Roxie! You're alive. Oh, sweetie, I was so worried. You're back! You're really back? Thank God. I'm on my way."

I made the next call to my father-in-law, Dad Wermuth, the second most important man in my life. "Dad, it's Roxie. I just woke up and had to call." Choking out the words through tears, I said, "I heard your prayer for me while I was in the coma and wanted to say thank you for telling me you loved me."

I am embarrassed to admit I did not want to return to my earthly body. When Uncle Paul told me to go back and I became aware of my life on earth and my precious family, I should have wanted to go back and reunite with them. Didn't I love them? Aren't they the most important thing, and shouldn't I have given up anything to be with them again?

I would have answered *yes* to all those questions. Yet all the love I had for my husband and daughters was not enough to make me want to go back. My sense of obligation to them couldn't compel me. Nor could any amount of pity I might have felt for their missing me. Heaven was too magnificent. And twelve years of bondage undone in a moment was too good to give up. I would never have willingly left heaven.

This place, or state of being, I had just walked through was vivid and tangible. It could not possibly have been a figment of my imagination. Everything I saw, heard, smelled, and touched pulsed with life more than anything had on earth. My father and Uncle Paul were more vibrant than they had ever been on earth. And I saw for myself that in God's heavenly presence there is no fear, no sadness, no suffering.

The feeling of running through the heavenly meadow was a bit like running through the old Mellish farm when I was a child. Its 300 acres seemed endless to me, and Uncle Paul always ran at my side. We laughed until my sides hurt. Both there and in heaven I felt happy and free. But in heaven Dad also ran along and gave me the attention I had craved all my life. And there were no boundaries of space or joy.

Around me now were windowless walls, only tolerable because of the ventilation system, and beeping machines to keep people like me alive.

Alive. I wasn't sure what that meant anymore.

Where I'd been, the seemingly endless tunnel opened to an endless expanse of beauty. No walled-in space limitations.

Everything, whether I saw or felt it, was infinite. Even that meadow of yellow flowers under a blue sky surpassed any sight on earth.

That place needed no ventilation system to keep things tolerable. I never noticed any weather per se. I had thought the brilliant light would be hot, yet it wasn't. And I didn't need sunscreen. The entire time I never sensed any wind, rain, change of temperature, or anything related to weather at all. Some of us like changing weather, and maybe other places and times in heaven have something like that. I only felt perfection in God's presence.

I never once thought of material things. I cannot even tell you what we were wearing. I only knew I was barefoot and had the hair of my dreams. The light of God saturated my entire body—and that light, that presence of God, is all we need. Material things as we know them on earth seemed to have no importance. My impression was that we will be too filled with the Spirit, too full of life, to be concerned with things so trivial.

What does it mean to be alive?

Earthly assumptions no longer held.

And yet…there obviously had to be more. As unmistakably as I experienced these things, I also sensed I had not seen heaven's fullness, did not fully enter it.

I didn't see God's throne or attending angels. I didn't see any other people besides Dad and Uncle Paul. And I didn't see any pearly gates, streets of gold, or whatever else I might have expected.

I wondered why. After thinking about it for weeks, I concluded that I may have been just outside heaven's gates. According to the medical records, as low and near to death as I was, it seemed my vital statistics had been normal; I had not officially died.

I learned that as the brain dies, neurons misfire, which is what scientists speculate may cause the typical visions of moving toward bright lights at the time of death or near death. But in my case that was impossible because I had been stable. And for a long time I saw a whole lot more than light.

Then the nature of my experience became as clear as I could grasp it.

I was in God's Waiting Room. That's the best term I can think of. In heaven but not completely.

Now it all made sense.

Still, that was much more than I could have possibly imagined or deserved. It was not my time to fully enter heaven. But God let me in His Waiting Room.

A mere glimpse of what was to come overwhelmed me. I believe that God allowed me this foretaste and saved the full splendor for when He would finally take me home to be with Him. I can hardly imagine how I'll take in heaven's full splendor.

I did not speak of this experience for months. I eventually spoke to my husband, and even that was limited. I could not talk much to anyone about this. It was so personal and intimate, a rare gift I wanted to protect. I feared that if I spoke of it, people would discount what had happened, and the gift God had given me would be unappreciated—or worse, rejected. Words cannot fully express what it's like to have a glimpse of heaven and feel God's presence. How could I possibly share an experience like this enough to allow people to comprehend the glory, serenity, and beauty of this place? I couldn't.

I finally found the strength to tell Dad Wermuth about my experience. He listened. I'll never forget that. Those two words mean so much to me: He listened. He told me to put this into writing before I forgot any of the details. I am so grateful for my father-in-law's convincing me to tell my story of this great gift.

Seeing God's eternal paradise for believers was not only a rare privilege, it was also a humbling experience I will cherish the rest of my life, the greatest gift I have ever received. Since this experience, many people have told me about other heaven experiences. As I read about them I was shocked at the similarities to my own. I never doubted my journey after that. It was real. More than that, heaven is real. In my youth, I sometimes had doubts, but no longer.

But why me? I do not know. I am imperfect and unworthy. I've made many mistakes, and I've never done great deeds for which God would give me a preview of heaven.

I believe that from the time I was born, He was preparing me for this entire journey. I'm grateful that He's given me an opportunity to testify about what I've experienced. I dedicate my life to Him and will do whatever He wants me to do.

I fulfilled my promise to care for Mom, who suffered from Alzheimer's for another two years. Her eyes that had once twinkled with love now fell into a blank stare. No more tender mother/daughter talks; no more laughter. Our only connection came when I fed her or when I held her and felt her soft, warm skin on mine. For me she had died the day she couldn't remember me anymore. And a part of me died too.

Yet after my visit to heaven, a peace rested on me as I visited her every day. The original sadness lifted because I had been to the place my mother would spend eternity.

At the end she had a severe stroke, and a week passed before she died. During those last days I stayed at the nursing home, where I sang hymns, read from the Bible, and reminded her of all the things she had done for me while I was growing up. Hospital staff watched me. One nurse said, "I didn't mean to disturb you, but I've never witnessed this kind of bond between a woman and her mother." Another time Mom had a fever, and I was washing her down with a cool rag and singing to her. Eight nurses and nurse's aides stood behind me crying.

Even simple actions done with God's love touch the hearts of other people.

Beyond fulfilling that promise, God seems to have had a greater purpose both in my going to Heaven's Waiting Room and in returning. My father and uncle took me into the meadow, where I received healing and sanctifying light. They told me I had more to do in my life and that I had to go back. I witnessed their happiness and experienced their love. What would have happened had they not met me? Perhaps that's not the right question because I believe God's purpose was for them to help me deliver His message that He loves us despite our sin and will welcome us into the glory of heaven if we turn to Him.

Thus He sent me back.

I have been told countless times that the light of God's presence radiates from me every time I tell about that moment.

It transformed me into who I am today. Both from pain and from ecstasy, we have so much to learn. I will try to express it.

Chapter 9

PAIN IN THE LIGHT OF HEAVEN

I consider that our present sufferings are not worth comparing with the glory that will be revealed in us (Romans 8:18).

My joy and message do not come without constant physical pain. Sometimes it consumes me. MS, especially chronic progressive, perpetually threatens. There is no cure, only medication to ease the discomfort. The plaques in the brain are in control. Depending on where they form, anything can happen, even paralysis or blindness, and death usually comes from complications like pneumonia.

I used to be scared every time a new symptom erupted. David and I would think, *This is it*. But the problem would miraculously pass or settle into a new obstacle. I am no longer afraid. Because I have seen heaven.

Not only have I stopped being afraid, I've come to accept my life for what it is and however it turns out. If God chooses to heal me, I accept His plan. If not, I will continue to dedicate my life to Him. He has filled me with a peace that surpasses all understanding.

I'm not a masochist, but if pain and suffering doesn't kill us, it will make us stronger. Overcoming obstacles is a universal challenge, but an even greater motivator. Overcoming an obstacle lifts our confidence and empowers our will to fight. That *will* is important, because many times I feel defeated when I can't do certain things as well as I used to.

Music is so important to me, especially playing my clarinet. In rehearsals at church I get down on myself because my fingers won't move as quickly as they used to, or my mind won't follow the notes as clearly and quickly as before. I feel stupid, and I begin talking negatively to myself. I get depressed. But by practicing three times harder than I did before MS, I overcome by memorizing the music and forcing my fingers to work with my brain, making a difficult passage a hard-won victory instead of a defeat.

In descending order of severity, my day-to-day symptoms are fatigue, depression, severe muscle spasms, numbness and tingling on my entire left side, cognitive difficulties, memory loss, difficulty walking, dizziness, mood changes, digestive problems, insomnia, vision distortions, and headaches. When I lose my balance, people think I've been drinking. It's so embarrassing.

Yet I do get a few perks that come with having a disability. One is the blue sign I can hang from my car's rear-view mirror that gets me a great parking spot. And at Disney World, where I went in a wheelchair, I got moved to the front of the line, along with my whole family. *Woohoo!* My favorite was when my oncologist invited David and me to attend a medical convention with her where the topic was on one of the medications I was taking. The keynote speaker (who also has MS) was a television star of one of my favorite shows, *Laverne and Shirley.* I approached him, star-struck and shaking, as I introduced myself. He said, "Well, Roxanne, MS looks really good on you." He got it! He ate dinner with us, and we talked all evening.

On the other hand, what a fortune I could amass if I collected a quarter for every time someone has said to me, "You look good, so you must be feeling good." *Ugh!* I leash my tongue and put on the smile-and-nod routine. If others could spend five minutes in my body, they'd know.

You can't see MS but oh, can you feel it. I often pretend to be happy and feel fine when I'm really not. Who wants to hear someone complain all the time? We all know people who characteristically lament about how they feel, and I don't want to be one. I have to keep some of my dignity!

The hardest thing to hide is the unpredictability of my condition. I can make plans with friends one minute and have to cancel the next because I have "crashed and burned." Sometimes people think I'm using my MS as an excuse, but that's the last thing I want to do.

The constant challenge is that since their initial onset, the symptoms have never let up, only progressed. In the beginning, I thought I would lose my mind. I have miraculously adjusted—or at least I try.

By all medical accounts I should be totally debilitated. My neurologist calls me his miracle patient because after so many years, I'm not only alive, I'm also not paralyzed. I do not take that for granted—especially when at the time of my diagnosis, the only person I knew with MS was quadriplegic.

In January 2012, my doctor was reviewing my chart at my regular six-month visit to his office. As he flipped through the pages, he asked, "How long have you been diagnosed with MS? Has it been four or five years?"

I looked at him dumbfounded because my doctor has such an impeccable memory. How could he not remember how long he had been my doctor? "Seventeen and a half."

Now it was his turn to be dumbfounded. He looked through my chart again, trying to find the date of my first office visit.

I said, "You won't find it there. I'm on my fifth chart."

He looked at David, eyes incredulous.

"Doctor, I was forty when you diagnosed me. I am now fifty-eight."

He looked at each of us, shook his head, and said, "I don't know what you are doing, but keep doing it." Advice from the expert.

What am I doing? I'm putting myself—everything I am and have—in God's hands. Once I gave myself completely to God, my life changed drastically. I went from being crushed under MS and wanting to die to wanting everything that life has to offer.

Faith has powered me through the hard times. It is my fuel to keep going, and on the right path. Faith also gives me an unending source of happiness and hope. And that keeps me going. Uncle Paul used to say, "Grass will never grow under Rox's feet." That's why friends have given me a nickname, "The Roxinator."

Many people say, "If she can get through that, and have a genuine smile on her face, then I can get through this."

What do you have to get through?

People ask if I'm mad at God. That's a normal thing to ask, but think about the logic: It's a negative approach to a negative situation. It easily happens when we presume that God's job is to make life nice and keep us happy—an idea totally alien to the Bible. And as we do, we bop through life as if God is just there on the side when we need Him or sitting in a church building to meet us on Sundays. We'll carry on like this until something bad happens—then get mad at God.

What do we expect out of life? Bad things will always happen. This isn't being negative; it's being real. It's far better to talk to God *before* trouble happens, when everything seems peachy—and to love Him not for what He gives us but for who He is to us. When that relationship becomes strong, it will sustain us through inevitable hard times. The heaven part of life comes *after* earth.

As time passes I gain new symptoms, reminders that MS is constantly invading my body. Is each new twitch, pain, or loss of ability an effect of MS or something else? Whatever the answer, the fears that seized me prior to my heaven experience no longer exist. Because I have seen heaven. And I can say it's more real than life on earth. I know God is with me, and I'm in His mighty hands. That is enough.

Then why do bad things happen to good people? Intellectuals to common folk have universally wrestled with that question for thousands of years. We all know they can happen for lots of reasons—and some of them only God knows. It's not my place to dive into that here. But like many others, I have seen what happens *behind* the bad news. What is God doing through them, because of them, or in spite of them?

I believe the answer is purpose. For whatever reason trouble happens, God will still do something good. Romans 8:28 again. It's true. In all things, both good and bad, God does work for the good of those who love Him and are called according to His purpose. Our part is to accept it and fulfill it.

It took me a while to reach this understanding. I now see what I mentioned earlier: God needed to catch me so He could slow me down and use me for something better.

God uses our personal experiences to help others. We are like threads that weave in and out of each others' lives, making changes and impact on people who need to hear our stories. I think this is why I enjoy quilting so much. A thread is insignificant by itself, a barely visible strand. But when combined with many more threads and colors, beautiful patterns develop, and they tell a story. I am convinced that we all have a purpose to fulfill and something beautiful to create as our story weaves with others'.

We all make choices when bad things happen, and these responses are based on how we prepare ourselves beforehand.

A sense of purpose can make a huge difference between wise and unwise choices.

What choices will you make?

Some ask if my MS is a punishment from God. This is an understandable question. But this conclusion has never entered my mind. This may sound weird, but I think God enabled me to get MS, and I mean *enabled*. My MS healed me from the person I used to be.

You might say that I got healed from being normal. Before MS I was consumed with image and accomplishment. I may have made my own hole in the ozone layer going through aerosol cans of hairspray, and in my corporate climbing I would have clawed through those holes if I could have. MS was a brick wall I crashed into, and in a matter of hours, my life changed. Now I wouldn't know what to do with hairspray, and I'd be happy even if I lived in a hole in the ground. Image and accomplishment no longer impress me. I'm done with normal.

Part of this healing comes from being humbled. I'm still highly motivated, but toward different priorities. I care less about myself and more about others, especially the elderly people in my church. The old Roxanne would have put her own agenda first and not tolerated the interruption of caring for seniors. Now I feel honored to bring them food, keep them company, and take them to the doctor. I spend a lot of my time at retirement homes. The seniors will say they are old, stuck there until they die, and have no worth. But they do have worth. I see one group of people who, for the most part, are Christians strong in their faith. I love to gather them and tell them about heaven. I also tell them it's a privilege to be with them because they have more life experience and maturity of faith than I do. And as they find their worth and purpose, they enter into a joy they'd once lost—or maybe never had.

Encouraging others affirms my own sense of purpose. And the cost to me is well worth it.

Daily life can be challenging, and sometimes I just want to rest for eternity. But I refuse to give in. I choose to push through the pain and depression. As I've struggled every day, I've been rewarded with hope. I expected to be totally paralyzed by now, yet I can still walk, sew, and cook supper. I am amazed.

I still have moments of darkness and thoughts of despair, but I'm not suicidal anymore. Thankfully those death desires are gone forever. I still need to take antidepressants for my illness, but usually the help of a good friend who just listens is all I need. My friendships are one of my greatest gifts, and I cherish them. Above all that, God has supernaturally sustained me, and joy is my strength.

If you were in my place, would you rather have a physical healing or a spiritual healing? God did a miracle in my body, but the miracle in my soul is greater.

What might He do in your life?

I've learned a new perspective on pain and trouble. I found what countless others have—that when I put adversity into God's hands, He makes positive things happen.

I don't go around feeling like a martyr. That would be no good to me or anyone else. The same way fasting reminds us to pray, my pain reminds me of how blessed I am with all I can still do. And because I maintain a positive attitude in the midst of my pain, others who carry their own are curious and more open to me. They want to know how I could possibly have any happiness facing a future like mine. And how I can be motivated to do all the things I do in spite of how exhausted I get.

Simply said, I have a passion that can't be extinguished. It's based on my faith and enlivened by my experience of heaven.

The more I talk with people, the stronger I get mentally, even as my body gets weary. And as my disease progresses, my faith and passion grow continually stronger. Something good happens to me each and every time I talk with people about heaven. It's almost as if I mentally re-enter heaven as I describe that journey. Whatever my mood may be, it changes for the better, and I tend to smile until my cheeks hurt. I am always growing and always seeking the positive in *every* situation. This is part of fulfilling God's purpose for me.

Everyone, and I do mean everyone, has adversities in life. And we all have some kind of positive experience that can similarly help us see bad things in a new way. Whether adversity is related to health, money, relationships, occupation, addictions, whatever, there is always a possibility for something positive. Though I still have MS, I'm miraculously alive and not in a wheelchair. I have bad days, but I have faith, hope, and purpose.

Adversity has taught me what's important. My father raised me to think that the important thing in life was a spotless house—not home, just house—along with the type of car I drive and the amount of money I earn. Like my father, I didn't want people to come into my home because I thought they would mess it up! Many times David asked me, "When your life is over, will you be proud that you kept a spotless house, had a great career, and drove a BMW, or will you be sad that you didn't spend more time with family and friends?"

I finally figured out the right answer. Facing daunting challenges so many times put earthly possessions and accomplishments in their rightful, bottom-of-the-list place.

By choosing to embrace adversity's lesson of what's important, I entered positive life change. Dad Wermuth said that when I was working I never had time for their side of the family. He said I show them more love now, take time with them, am more understanding, and have reprioritized from success to principles. Mom said I used to be self-centered and jealous but am now much happier and even exude the light of Christ from my face.

I also understood that without adversity, I wouldn't grow. I hated many of the lessons, but because I endured and chose to open my heart and mind, the benefits changed not only my life but other people's as well.

When David and I had been married for about five years, I was four months pregnant with our second child. We were excited until I began having labor pains. I went to the hospital and into labor for more than seven hours, after which I delivered a stillborn boy. The nurse let me hold him, and he fit into the palm of my hand. I was sent home the next day without any examination, and a couple of days later I began labor again. Before I could reach the hospital, I delivered the afterbirth. One of the nurses had the nerve to ask, "What did you do to make God angry enough to take your baby?" Can you believe it? I was horrified. Someone in my family said, "What's the big deal? She's young; she can have another baby." Oh, that hurt, and I will remember those jabs for the rest of my life.

From that I grew to understand the emotional and physical pain others experience—whatever it may be. If we don't go through adversity, how can we possibly understand others who do—even if their problems are their own fault? We tend to judge them instead. That doesn't help anyone.

Once I was driving home from the store and something told me to stop at a friend's house. I really wanted to get home because my soap opera was about to come on. Yet I could not shake this feeling, maybe a nudge from God? So I stopped in—and I'm not one who likes unannounced visits.

My friend came to the door. Her arms were shaking, and she stared at me with wide, teary eyes. "How did you know?"

Know what? I paused. "I really didn't know, but here I am."

She invited me in, and there lay a shotgun behind a sofa pillow. She confessed that she had pointed it at her head and was about to pull the trigger. Then she heard my knock.

We had a long talk. And because of how I'd grown from my own painful past, I was able to empathize with her and understand her issues. That's what she needed. She went on to get help, let God work in her life, and is now living happily.

What would have happened if I had not learned from my adversities? If I had ignored the feeling to stop to see my friend? If I had not learned to be empathetic? What if I had just thrown Christian platitudes at her—repent, have faith, and you'll be fine—rather than spending time to listen and understand? Again, God's purpose. Are you using painful life experiences to help others, or are you covering up and trying to look good?

I had to lose everything to gain *everything*.

I tried to prove to my dad I could make it big, and the perfectionist world he raised me in convinced me I had to perfect my life. My driven-ness allowed no time for family, friends, or God. After MS I argued with my neurologist to just give me a pill so I could continue my obsessions. My company manager kindly had to end my career. It was like death to me.

Then that death gave me a new life I never could have had otherwise.

MS freed me from my rat race. My priorities changed. My focus changed. I saw something I could never have seen before: I had to lose everything to gain *everything*.

When I lost the high-powered top sales rep spot, I "achieved" humility. The alarm to start my daily corporate race stopped ringing. Against my will I lay in bed, watched TV, and read books. My designer suits and trendy heels gathered dust in the closet. Instead I got sweat suits and sensible shoes. My newfound view from below opened a door to a world that had always been there, but I could not see it, and never would have imagined it, until I was forced.

Without a career to chase and an image to maintain, my life simplified. When I lost everything, God replaced what I lost with so much more than I had before.

I became part of my family in ways I never had before. We spent more time together, worked in the yard, and explored new hobbies. I gained an even better house than I previously had, handicapped accessible and on my grandfather's land. I spent valuable time with David's aging parents. I learned to live wisely.

I grew to see through the superficiality of the world we all live in because I slowed down. During previous years I thought I saw life's priorities just fine. MS freed me to see how blind I really was.

I do not want my story's focus to be on my disease or pain or suffering. Rather, I want to tell my story as it flourishes because of my disease.

Instead of becoming embarrassed or discouraged when I struggle with my balance, I've learned to rejoice that I can still walk. At times I may need a cane, walker, or wheelchair, but I can walk. Painful muscle spasms have become reminders that I'm still alive and God's sustaining me.

I never thought of myself as beautiful, yet people often tell me I am—even though I'm bald. *Ha-ha* to the truckloads of hairspray I once expended to make my thin hair poufy. Few things are more humbling to a woman than having a bad hair day. The Bible even describes a woman's hair as her crowning glory. Well, not for me! I'm now content to observe that God gave me a nicely shaped head!

Focusing on God and where He leads me is far more important—and rewarding—than anything I achieved or acquired before MS. So of course I have no interest in receiving anyone's pity. Rather I feel blessed, and I have everything I could want.

I'm happy beyond anything I imagined during the years I chased false happiness. I've learned to pursue love, understanding, and serving others. Most important, I want to be God's follower and tell people that He's real, He loves you, and He's waiting for you. He's prepared a place for you, and from what I've seen, you won't want to miss it.

Like many children, I had to decide at an early age to fight for myself or be crushed under the blows of adults. We all have some kind of pain and some kind of choice to make. And our choices determine our life's story. We can't control what other people write into our story. But we *can* choose what *we* write. We must. No matter what happens to us, we still direct how our story turns out. Will you cower in the dark corner of your life's struggles, or will you come out swinging?

The heaven experience that once made me not want to come back to earth has now made me never want to go back to my life before MS. And I'm not crazy.

I look back on my healthy body, achievements, money, fancy car, dream house, popularity—the kinds of things most people either want or toil to get. Given the choice of having all that back, *and being the person I was*, versus a body racked with debilitating disease, I'll keep the diseased body.

Despite the trinkets of success, my soul was sick. Possessions and achievements blinded me to the life that God opened up because of my suffering. God healed me from the self-centered person I was—a spiritual healing. Going from ICU to Heaven's Waiting Room truly felt as if part of me died and was reborn. I am alive in God's Spirit and make it my mission to share my faith daily. Prior to MS I never knew peace or happiness to this degree.

If anyone doubts my heaven experience, and I know there will be those doubters, I have an answer for that. Even if it were all a dream—which it wasn't—look at what happened because of it.

Every aspect of my life has changed. My faith in God gets stronger every day. My passion continues to grow. And I have no more fear of the unknown. Hundreds of people have heard my story, and in the end the responses are the same: They have a renewed hope for their own lives as well as for loved ones they've lost. There's far too much impact on reality for heaven to have been a dream.

So is my MS really a disability? Or is it a new ability?

Chapter 10

LIFE IN THE LIGHT OF HEAVEN

Now the Lord is the Spirit, and where the Spirit of the Lord is, there is freedom. And we, who with unveiled faces all reflect the Lord's glory, are being transformed into his likeness with ever-increasing glory, which comes from the Lord, who is the Spirit (2 Corinthians 3:17–18).

I remember the demonic presence that spoke to me after the college revival service the night David and I decided to marry, and how it said, "You think your life will be easy since God called you two to be together. But I promise you, it won't. I will make it as hard as I can for you."

That turned out to be true. Whatever that demon (or whatever it was) did, I don't know. But I didn't handle it well. Before MS I lived a blatantly double life of good person/bad person. After MS I consumed myself with self-pity.

When I was first diagnosed with MS, I was afraid I wouldn't live long. So I started writing a daily journal. Mostly I wrote as if I were composing letters to our girls, telling how they had added so much love to my life. But later when I re-read the journals, I discovered that I had focused on my disability. Too many entries were depressed accounts of suffering in bed and hoping it would all come to an end. I held no hope. If I read those old journals now, they appear as if someone else wrote them. I can hardly believe the sadness that drips from page after page.

How selfish I was all those times I tried, or just wanted, to end my life. I was so obsessed about myself that I hurt everyone around me. And I played with my eternity the same way I nearly killed myself.

Whatever would have happened to me, I would have also missed the countless blessings God has showered on me in this life. More important, I would have denied many people their opportunities to bless me. The more we say "no, thank you" to people who offer help, the more we rob their own blessings. So many people have expressed happiness at the chance to bring me meals and gifts or visit me in the hospital, bring me to the doctor, or just help me through a door or up the stairs.

One cold and icy Sunday following the morning church service, I struggled across the slippery parking lot toward my car. It was shortly after being diagnosed, and I had a difficult time walking even without ice. A kind man from our church not only offered to help me to my car, he offered to drive me home too. I got angry at him and shouted, "I'm not some little ole lady needing assistance! Leave me alone."

So many things are different now. Or rather, they're the same; I am different. After going to heaven, I've had a personality transplant. The old Roxanne has disappeared and been replaced by a new person with a new heart. Spiritually I've climbed, even soared, higher than I ever dreamed possible, and I did *not* have to claw my way there. Surprisingly it seems almost effortless now that God slowed me down and healed me from being normal—and after I gave myself totally over to Him. I'm not getting in His way anymore.

Now instead of beating other people down in order to pass them by, I'll grab on to them and take them with me. My new goal is to share my joy, which in the present brings peace and in the future brings hope.

People who knew me years ago have said, "That doesn't sound like the Roxanne I knew." It doesn't sound like the one I knew either. And I will never stop growing as a person.

When I think of that dark spirit now, I can laugh. Because I've won. Never again will I let the darkness overshadow me.

One seemingly small thing that my joy has changed is my name preference. When I was young I pleaded with my mother to not call me Roxie, especially in front of David. To me it had an unsophisticated, childish tone. But my whole family called me Roxie anyway. Now I know myself as a child of God and *want* to be called Roxie. Since visiting God's Waiting Room, I often reach my arms to God as a child would reach for her parent to pick her up and hold her safely in strong arms. I will always be His child. I will forever be Roxie.

You might wonder if I have a rainbows-and-butterflies life now that I have seen heaven. The answer is *no!* I face struggles like anyone else and will continue to have struggles till the day I die. The difference is that I now have a strong faith and see life clearly. This is where joy makes the big things happen.

I will face problems for the rest of my life. One big one has caused David and me unbearable stress, sadness, and disbelief in a situation we never thought we'd have to deal with in our lifetime— the loss of a loved one to drug addiction. The experts told us we had to walk away and turn our backs. But I couldn't let go. For years we've been brokenhearted and broken financially. My problem was that I desperately tried to fix the situation myself. After years of failure I was finally able to turn my back. "Let go and let God," as I've been told. Negative as all this is, the positive is that I've now let go and am praying daily for this lost soul. The sadness is sometimes unbearable, but God has promised me it is now in His hands. "Stop worrying, daughter," He seems to tell me. "I am carrying her now and have great plans for her future." This is a deep comfort to me and gives me the peace I need.

Like most other people on the planet, the older I get, the faster time seems to pass. The difference for me now is that I don't see my life coming to an end. I am overwhelmed with joy as I imagine going back to heaven and beginning a new life. How much happier can I get?

So of course I don't fear death. Once my purpose on earth is done, I look forward to what's beyond. I've got hope and lots more to share.

People often avoid or deny things they find scary, mysterious, or beyond ordinary life. So it's no surprise that most people evade thinking about death and the afterlife. And when they do, it's often too late. Even when people are not afraid of dying, I think part of the reason they put off the thought is that they're only concerned about the here and now, and they assume they'll have time to think about death later. Even smart people do this.

The first time I saw my dentist after I was diagnosed, he asked the routine question if I had any changes in my health. I told him about my MS diagnosis.

He showed true compassion the way he lowered his clipboard and said, "I am so sorry."

I said, "Don't be sorry for me."

He looked confused.

"My disease doesn't make me so different from anyone else."

"What do you mean?"

"Your life could end before mine. You could get into a car accident and never make it home tonight."

"You're right. I never thought of it that way."

Life is unpredictable, and none of us knows how much time we have left on earth. That puts us all on a level playing field. Whether you're healthy or not, you still need to be ready.

When I was confronted with my own mortality, I started to think differently. I came to believe and experience that each day in itself is a gift. I discovered I have a daily choice to ignore it or recognize it.

Each day in turn reveals its own special gift. When I wake in the morning, I anticipate what blessing I might receive. And one always comes to me—it could be an act of kindness or cookies from a neighbor; or it could be a new realization or appreciating newly blooming flowers. Do you recognize the daily gifts that come to you?

Previously I didn't experience each day's gifts because I wasn't looking. I was too preoccupied. Now that I no longer live in a pressure cooker, I'm not conned into thinking I must achieve and possess. I have the peace and mental space to discover the good things that continually come my way.

One day when I was down because of my drug-addicted loved one, I decided to pull myself together and go down to my waterfall and pull weeds. They were thick, tall, and thorny. As I labored and struggled on the slippery rocks, I noticed a purple lily among the weeds. Its beauty made me stop and think. It was God's gift to me that day, and I was grateful.

David and I have both learned to see these kinds of things, and our days are now filled with laughter and love. I'm also making up for all I put him through! Yes, we still have plenty of struggles, but with our faith sustaining us, we rejoice in the time we have together.

Making new friends and talking with people each day gives me a joy similar to what I felt at Christmas when I was a child, especially the year I received twelve pencils, individually wrapped by my dear mother. Twelve individually wrapped pencils may not seem like much, but I considered the effort it took my mother to wrap up all those pencils. Sometimes the small things in life rise as our biggest, and happiest, memories.

The big lesson I've learned on daily living is this: Seek out possibilities in your day. Even though you may face adversity, decide right then what you'll do about it. Choose with hope and faith to be positive. If you've done wrong, repent and be forgiven. Remember that God has promised to work for good in the lives of those who love Him and are called according to His purpose. Don't squander your time like I did after being diagnosed. My year-long pity party was a waste. Great possibilities await every one of us. To do nothing positive with our lives is a big waste of our earthly time. Because God gave us the gift of life and each day to live it, wouldn't He be disappointed if we threw it away? Grab on to something you can hope in, and fight with all your might. And if you die in the process, you'll get an upgrade to heaven! How bad can that be?

I have no fears now. *Peace* is the first word that comes to mind when I think of how my life has changed since I have been to heaven. Despite the sinister shadow MS casts, I feel blissful about life. It's in God's hands.

Life on earth can be like walking on a high wire. Since visiting heaven, I feel as though God is my safety net. Whatever life brings me, He will catch me when I fall. This is the best way I can describe the peace I feel.

Two of my greatest fears before my heaven experience were fear of heights and water. Now it is David who gets scared for my own lack of fear. What a change. I now enjoy canoeing, because I don't fear the water, and I love the tall bluffs when we vacation in Michigan's Upper Peninsula. I get so close to the edge for a clear view of God's beauty that David yells at me to get back. The only thing stopping me now is my limited ability to walk.

I can see past both good and bad times because I know that everything on this earth is temporary and eternity is bright, literally.

I don't fear death because I know I will continue to live in my spirit. Death is the ending of one phase of life and the beginning of another. Until then each day my thoughts are on the beauty, joy, and perfection that await me.

Think how wonderful it would be to cradle that happiness in your heart every single day, even in hardship. Wouldn't that alone be worth getting more acquainted with God?

I no longer worry about life's unpredictability. It doesn't matter. The only thing that matters is that we are always ready at any given moment to go home to the presence of our heavenly Father.

In my power-driven career days, one of my dominant traits was impatience—followed naturally by frustration when I didn't get my way quickly enough. I learned well from my father. Clothes on the floor or crumbs on the counter sent me into a fit of yelling. How could my husband be so disrespectful? How dare those girls? A dirty dish left in the sink was an act of spiteful disregard toward me. When things were as I liked them, I had my mother's gentle nature, but Dad's venom was always waiting to burst through.

Since heaven I've learned to be peaceful. No more Tasmanian devil in the house. I've realized how lonely life would be in an empty house with no crumbs to wipe. I've learned to love the people who make those messes rather than drive them away with my anger. I've grown to quietly smile and clean. Or I have fun. David always, and I mean always, leaves empty cereal boxes on the counter. Instead of henpecking, I quietly place the boxes under his pillow. Instead of yelling when the clothes hamper is left out of place and in my way, I deviously smile and place the hamper on top of the toilet. David, or any other culprit, receives the message with laughter.

Maybe I've gone a little crazy. Because now I even go out and help elderly people by cleaning their crumbs, clothes, and dishes. The old Roxanne would never have had time for anything so mundane. Now cleaning like this gives me continual chances to bless my family and others. And as I bless them, I feel blessed.

Wiping and washing have become times to listen to God. And I often sense His guidance as I do these humdrum tasks. Occasionally He prompts me to go help somewhere, give something, or encourage someone. When I follow through on this, the recipient is often overwhelmed by my generosity. But I tell them it's by God's leading. Giving from a joyful, peaceful heart is its own reward.

I've always loved my husband. Sort of. I had loving feelings in the whole mix of our life together. But it wasn't much of a romance. The love that overwhelmed me in youth was itself overwhelmed by my own greed. I took David for granted and shoved him aside.

My sickness dug that hole to a sometimes-fathomless depth. I put him and the girls through so much grief. Because I still loved him, I wanted to spare him the burden of a debilitated wife, so I begged him to divorce me. He deserved better.

I know people who have left their spouses due to serious illness. It wasn't what they had signed up for, and they didn't want to be burdened with a decrepit spouse. I understand this. Hiking through the woods and twirling at a wedding dance get traded for blue hand-icapped signs and pushing a wheelchair. Some people don't have that big an embrace. And they run.

But David said, "Would you leave me if I were the one who got sick?" That stopped me. Of course I would take care of him. I think. Would the old Roxanne have thought that way? I wasn't sure. I'm so different now I hardly know my old self.

I am overwhelmed at the love and dedication my husband has shown me during the past two decades. It's unconditional, the kind we vow at the altar: "in sickness and in health, till death do us part." We made it through hard times in which a lot of people sadly quit and separate to spare themselves that pain. Staying with someone through horrific problems, especially when the grief goes on for years, deepens and cements the relationship as nothing else can.

Since heaven I've come to believe that our marriage was ordained by God. I see God's purpose for giving David to me and me to him. Our bond is truly sacred to me. I've grown to cherish my husband, treasure him, even revere him. And as different as my bubbly and his calm personalities are, we know with amazing harmony how each other thinks and feels.

To express the love story that has become our marriage after my glimpse of heaven, here is an excerpt of a letter I wrote to David:

> My Dearest, my Love, my Forever…and a Day,
>
> I fell in love with you when we were only twelve. My mother told me that God had made a special boy for me who would someday be my husband. It was you, my love. I hold so many memories of you close in my heart. Do you remember helping plant thousands of pine trees with my family on the old farm up north? You wore a dark green shirt with fringe and took it off because you got too warm. I sat in the car, lifted that shirt to my nose, and breathed you in.

We've been together more than thirty-five years, and you've given me two beautiful girls. With God our Father being in the center of our lives, we have endured the hard times and become stronger. I feel your love deep into my heart, spirit, and soul. We have truly become one. I thank God every day I look into your eyes. You have loved me through all my shortcomings and my illness. You are my rock. I don't know how life would have ever been this sweet without you.

God has been so good to us through the years. There is nothing missing. David, you were my gift from Him, and the girls too. I have a heart big enough to hold all three of you.

For the rest of my life, I am committed to God and you.

Forever…and a day! That's how long I will love you!

Roxie

David wrote in response:

Roxie Sweetheart,

All I want in life is to hold you in my arms and to know you love me. You are the only one I have ever wanted to spend my life with, and that will never change. I just want you to know that there is one earthly thing you can always count on, and it is my love for you. We can handle any storm together.

I love you! Forever…and a day.

David

Of course people can love like this without ever going to heaven. But love like this is a reflection of God's love and brings a bit of heaven into our lives here and now. For all of us then, loving this way can become something we learn, experience, and share with another.

Life is so rich when lived in the light of heaven. And that richness is not solitary—it's shared with others and with God, as if we're all woven together.

Life to me is like a quilt that evolves in the sewing and has a unique story. Quilts are made of thousands of threads that weave in and out of each other, changing patterns and color schemes as they go. We are like threads in a quilt that weave in and out of each other's lives, and in the process we change and grow. How boring life would be if it were all one color and one pattern.

My favorite quilt pattern is "Flowers of the Bible" by Helen Curtis. I selected twelve flowers but could not bring myself to ignore the others in the pattern book, so I made a second quilt. The book identifies each flower's origin and distinction during Bible times. The most challenging pattern was the spiked-thorn detail of the Crown of Thorns flower. As I worked at it for weeks, I couldn't help but continually think of God's sacrifice and love for us.

So quilting weaves my life with God. Which is why it's my main hobby.

The numbness on my left side extends all the way to my fingertips, which can cause trouble. I've often finished sewing for the day only to find that I've sewn the quilt to my fingers. The first time I was horrified. Imagine pulling the quilt off your lap and realizing it's stuck on something, and the something is your other hand. Now it's happened so many times I've grown to laugh whenever it does. Pushing the needle then pulling the thread through my fingers really does look as bad as it sounds. And I've become an expert at cleaning blood. Even then I leave a lot of DNA behind on my quilts!

Flowers and quilting. I soon decided to take them to the next step—my head.

Chapter 11

FLOWERS OF HEAVEN

Flowers appear on the earth; the season of singing has come (Song of Songs 2:12).

I kept thinking about flowers. And I asked myself, "Why did I only see yellow flowers in heaven when the world has countless types, and even the Bible records many?" This was a challenge for me to understand until I was driving down a road one day and saw a meadow of yellow flowers. I screamed with excitement!

I found out they're called buttercups. I think they were God's way of reminding me of what He's given me and what is yet to come.

My thoughts often went back to my grandparents' farm, where Grandma had hundreds of flowers around the farmhouse. As a child I picked bouquets for her whenever I spent the weekend. The woods behind the farm yielded still more flowers. And I filled my little hands with bunches of them too—all presents for Grandma.

Staying with my grandparents was a spiritual experience. Grandpa was a preacher but made so little money that he also ran this farm with his sons. After breakfast he read the Bible to us, then we got on our knees and prayed in turn. My family didn't pray at home so I was afraid I'd sound stupid. But Grandpa and Grandma were happy with my attempts.

To me, the flowers around the house and in the woods somehow embodied their spirituality. Years later I remembered Grandma's flowers and found that some were similar to, and others the same as, the flowers of the Bible I'd quilted.

From Genesis to Revelation, the Bible is full of symbolic color meaning. God seems to love color. He invented it. After reading about flowers in the Bible and making quilts of them, I decided to go with God's variety of colorful flowers and step beyond quilting.

After my pre-heaven chemotherapy and hair loss, what grew back was never more than thin patches. So I had the choice of looking like an atomic bomb victim or wearing a wig. I had at least twenty of them for when I went out. But in warm weather or for long periods they were unbearable.

I tried everything from thickening shampoos to colored powder to hide my scalp. But I couldn't do anything with hair that was not there.

Then one of my friends came down with Alopecia, an autoimmune disorder that causes total hair loss. The devastation to her sense of identity and the embarrassment of baldness overwhelmed her until she couldn't even get out of bed. How could I help her? I knew exactly what she was going through. So we held each other. A lot.

Then I thought of something I could do to support her. I shaved my head.

She could hardly believe I did that.

And I could hardly believe I liked being bald. But it was better than a head of fuzz patches that made me feel old and ugly.

Shaving it all off was a way to take matters into my own hands. Neither chemo nor heredity nor a disease forced my hand. This was *my* choice. I felt empowered.

I also felt liberated. My razor cut off the sad reminders that I never had thick, bouncy hair. In their place I got a shiny scalp, the work of my own hands. So I regularly shaved my head.

But when I went out of the house bald, I felt naked. What to do?

My friend with Alopecia supported me in return and encouraged me to accept my lack of hair. Even to embrace it. Then do something positive with it.

As I wondered what that might be, I often remembered God's variety of flowers in heaven, in the Bible, and in my own yard. I wanted to make my experience of heaven count for something. And I had a whole head that needed covering. For more than a year I toyed with the idea of getting a tattoo. Flowers of heaven. On my head.

No, don't do it!—Why not? Well...

Yes. If God let me lose my hair, He at least gave me a nicely shaped dome for artwork. And I wanted my story to encourage people. They needed something to start the conversation.

No. David said, "Absolutely *not!*" then read me Leviticus 19:28, "Do not cut your bodies for the dead or put tattoo marks on yourselves. I am the Lord." He seriously cautioned me. "Think about it Roxie, no good Nazarene lady would get tattoos on her head! It's just a phase; you'll get over it. Please do not do this."

I prayed and carefully thought about this for a year. And I studied Leviticus 19:28. That verse actually seemed to address the practices of Israel's neighboring cultures, where people cut and tattooed themselves as part of mourning for the dead. I wasn't mourning anybody. If I got a tattoo, it would be for the glory of God. I've heard some argue that the tattooing wasn't related to the dead. But even if that's so, the verses both before and after this have to do with the Israelites distinguishing themselves from what their pagan neighbors did. My neighbors in Michigan are quite different from Israel's.

On the other hand, Isaiah 44:5 talks about writing "The Lord's" on your hand as an act of dedication. I figured I had more open space around my head than I did on my hand—all the more dedication.

Whether I was right or wrong, I believe that if God had not wanted me to put flowers on my head, He would have convicted me of my sin. He never did. This was a serious and permanent undertaking—done for a purpose. If I was wrong, I begged His forgiveness.

Finally the time came.

David went on a two-week canoe trip. I went to downtown Lapeer.

There are two tattoo shops in downtown Lapeer. I chose the one in a "friendly" area next to restaurants and quaint shops. The exterior looked bright, clean, and inviting. Pictures of tattoos hung in the window for all to see and presumably admire.

I parked my little yellow car outside the shop and sat there for a while, shaking from nerves. *This will be permanent, Roxie. Are you sure?* Yes. *Really, really sure?* No!

Okay, I'll just get out of the car, walk in the shop, and casually look around. No harm in that.

I opened the door, stepped in, and froze.

Skulls. Flames. Bizarre symbols. The walls were covered with designs.

Tattoo…um…*artwork,* apparently.

On a far wall was a spray-painted woman, naked on top with spider legs for her bottom half. Display cases overflowed with metal, lots and lots of metal, for more types of body piercing than I could imagine.

Heavy metal music blasted and seemed to pulse through my whole body. I did not want to pulse. Shock started setting in. I couldn't believe the words I was hearing. I thought those kind of lyrics were illegal.

And there were people. With tattoos. Like camouflage. Arms and legs and chests and backs and necks, even their faces.

They did have hair—in dreadlocks. Or Mohawks. One was shaved clean, maybe so he'd have more space for tattoos.

They had body piercings with enough dangling jewelry to overheat a metal detector. I didn't even know you could pierce cheeks, foreheads, the back of a neck, and oh my, a huge round thing under one guy's lower lip, expanding it into a mini basketball hoop. What kind of aliens were these?

I closed my eyes. The people were real, but maybe I had imagined the wall displays. Where were the pretty things like flowers, rainbows, and butterflies? I looked again at the walls. Yep. The same images were still there—skulls, flames, snakes, dragons, and the naked woman-spider.

I certainly did not feel warm and happy the way I had when entering heaven. This was closer to the gates of hell. And it occurred to me that I—a middle-aged, proper lady—didn't belong there. What was I thinking? My heart jackhammered. I felt suddenly weak. My mind said, *run!*

Run. That was difficult with MS. Okay, just look normal and nonchalantly walk out.

I turned to leave—

"Hi there!"

Oh, God, save me! I looked.

A young guy gave me a welcoming smile that lit up the room. Odd, because his face was completely tattooed and covered with piercings. His earlobes hung in big open circles with African-tribal-looking-ear-stretcher thingies.

Oh my.

He approached me.

Please don't.

"How can we help you?"

I smiled. Refroze. Leaked a nervous *he-he*. "Ah. Well. I'm not sure why I came here today…. Uh…I was sort of thinking of getting a tattoo. But maybe I'll think about it for a while." I turned again to leave.

"Come in and look around."

You've got to be kidding. I stood still.

"So, what were you thinking to have done?"

I looked at the door and let it stay shut. With me inside. *What am I doing?*

I explained why I was there and what I had in mind.

As if by itself my voice grew animated. And a half dozen curious, smiling employees gathered around me. The more I spoke, the more they encouraged me: "We admire you for not hiding." "You'll be our first woman who's asking for this." "We'll design something perfect just for you." They spoke kindly, and they didn't judge me the way I had judged them.

Though all seemed capable, they agreed my case wouldn't require just any tattoo artist; this would require someone with special skills.

Someone skilled in scalps.

Ed.

He was already approaching me. Late twenties, shaved head with tattoos all over, including his face, but no ear-stretcher thingies—that was good. He smiled and said, "Hello. What did you have in mind?"

My Indy 500 heart began to slow at his soft-spoken voice. He listened carefully as I told him my ideas.

Sketching preliminary designs on paper, he transformed my thoughts into artwork, and two days later the painstaking, year-long process began.

My head spun and my body shook. Would this hurt? Would I get some awful disease from having dirty needles jabbed in my skin? Would my doctor be mad? Would David be mad?

I lay face down on a massage table and saw how clean Ed's tennis shoes were. That brought me relief. As I watched his knee bounce up and down as he worked, my fears began to fade. I felt safe. And despite some of their vocabulary, the people in the shop all spoke and acted with kindness.

For an hour and a half the furious needle of the tattoo gun rat-a-tat-tatted me. Like the left side of my body, some parts of my head were mercifully numb. Other parts were not. By the end I was in such pain I felt nauseated. Ed asked me to sit up slowly so I wouldn't pass out. He was holding a mirror and smiling. "Want to take a look?"

My nerves went wild again. I looked.

Oh my. Though just a beginning, it was so beautiful I cried. Over and over I said, "How beautiful." After all these years I felt complete, fully clothed, and pretty. Then I hugged the tattooist.

People on the sidewalks gave me two thumbs up and several commented how beautiful the artwork was. I smiled and thanked them. *I'm cool! I'm hip! I'm no longer an old bald lady!*

But as I drove home, I cried over what I had done behind my husband's back while he was away. He called that evening, and I cried some more and confessed I'd done something I'd promised not to do. "Yes, David, I got a tattoo on my head." At least he felt relieved it wasn't something worse.

I returned to the shop for many more sessions. Ed was always calm, comforting, and understanding. He never tried to talk me into anything. As I became one of the regulars, he even changed the music to something tamer when I came in.

As he pricked and inked, I told him my story, including my trip to heaven, and how I felt naked without my hair. He listened carefully and asked many questions: "What was it like up there?"—Beautiful beyond description.—"You mean I won't remember my wife or daughter if I die first?"—There won't be time to remember, and no space in our minds for anything not in heaven.—"How could I not remember all the people I have known and cared about in my lifetime?"—This agitated him, and whenever he became uneasy, his leg jiggled up and down, which made me nervous because my head was in his hands. But as the months passed, we became good friends.

Despite my differences from the denizens of the tattoo parlor, they all welcomed me and made me feel normal. *Normal!* They not only respected me for doing something positive with my baldness, they respected me for my firm stand on faith. And they took care of me: "Do you need some water, Roxie?" "Do you need a snack?" "How are you feeling?" What a great bunch of people. I came to know all of them well. I even got to *like* them.

It took one year of nineteen sessions, totaling about 40 hours, for Ed to complete his work. Though the scalp is one of the most sensitive areas to tattoo, most of the time I could only feel the vibration of the instrument puncturing my head with thousands of ink-filled needle jabs. But occasionally Ed hit a spot that curled my toes. One time they had to carry me to a chair where I could recuperate before driving home.

After having the initial yellow flowers inked, I had Ed incorporate the flowers of the Bible and Grandma's garden, which I suspect are in heaven, but I haven't yet seen there.

We started on my left side with lilies of the valley, but my body rejected the white ink. Each flower blistered, bubbled, and burst. White ink oozed out along with puss. Scabs formed and eventually healed. Try number two replaced them with bluebells, which worked.

Next to them came pink lilies, then on top in the back the purple coneflower. David and I planted a wildflower meadow at the front of our property, and this beautiful flower comes up every year.

Below that we put a special one—the morning glory. Morning glories wound around the dinner bell my mother once rang to call her brothers in from the field for dinner. I loved the tendrils that wind their way into spirals. At the bottom came another in our wildflower meadow, the pink phlox.

To the right of the morning glory we put the purple-and-yellow pansy, which is meaningful to me because I was called this name in my early media career. But the pansy is one tough flower. It often keeps blooming through the winter snow. Under the pansy came the bluish purple crocus that sprouts through the snow in early spring. Last, from behind my right ear across my neck, we placed the bleeding heart, which looks like its name and depicts the way God's heart bleeds for us when we stray from Him and the way Jesus bled on the cross for the love of humanity.

I left the front-right part of my head with no tattoos. People ask me if I'll ever get that part done as well. My answer is no. I want to see the blank section of my head to remind me that I am a work in progress. I will never be finished or perfect. I will keep growing in my faith and as a person for the rest of my life.

Being with these people brought to mind the times my younger daughter, Sara, brought her friends to church. They wore ratty clothes and smelled of cigarettes and pot. One used the church bathroom to clean up because he was homeless. Sara taught me not to judge them. Because I so often did. She continually reminded me of my judgmental nature and reminded me to look beyond appearances and into their hearts.

Sometimes people need a kick in the rear, but they also need an embrace. So many people have pain and heartaches in their lives. Some put up nice exteriors; others get obviously messed up. No one benefits when we judge them for how they handle their lives. But everyone can benefit when we listen and try to understand. Each instance opens the opportunity to lift up.

As I encounter people with different lifestyles, I've learned to find the good in them. And even if I still don't like them, I won't be disrespectful.

Some Christians may judge me, but the Bible does say, "Go into all the world and preach the good news to all creation" (Mark 16:15). That includes stepping out of our comfort zones and connecting with people who are different from us. People we would otherwise avoid. Or hate.

Though I freaked out at the weird-looking tattooed people, they heard what I had to say. I learned to look past their exteriors—their packaging—to what was inside them. They were kind. These people became like my second family.

I still drop by the tattoo shop to say hi or bring them lunch. Their world and mine are not the same, but they intersect. And despite our differences, I love these people.

I know what it feels like when people make negative statements about my tattoos and me. It hurts. But in the end, they can think what they want. I know there's a place in heaven reserved for me. I stepped out and did something crazy. I became a walking bill-board for my experience and the hope of what I believe in. How many people do you know who every single day get asked a question that opens the door to talking about heaven? That's my point. I am willing to talk every day about the miracle that awaits us when we die—if we are prepared.

Ed's tattoo art turned my desires into a reality around my head. I no longer felt naked. In the past I was so pathetically vain, I cried rivers over slowly and gradually losing my hair when I was young.

Now I'm glad I did. It was the best thing for me. I—feel—free. On top of that I gained a conversation starter to tell people what I experienced.

The flowers inked on my head are an expression of what God inked on my heart. When I tell people about it, in person or through this book, I hope they will hear me from deep in their own hearts. And I hope they will have their own unique spiritual experiences that change them and grow them to overcome what they're facing.

One day I was in downtown Lapeer, without my wig, leaving the local drugstore as a young man was about to enter. He was tall and intimidating, his arms were full of tattoos (called sleeves), and he had those awful ear globes.

As he passed, he said, "Hey, aren't you the lady who went to heaven?"

"Um…yes. That's me." I was shocked. It was the first time anyone had ever asked.

A recovering drug addict, he insisted he had to talk. His wife and children had left him, but he had to support them. He said he believed in God but needed confirmation that He was real. He wanted to hear all about heaven, everything I saw, felt, and heard. He desperately needed to know that there was a God who listened when he prayed.

It was 100 degrees outside. Bad for MS. I could tell he didn't want to inconvenience me, yet he was desperate to talk.

As I responded to his questions, his face lit up with hope and enthusiasm. He smiled and thanked me profusely. But it was God who used me.

This was a good reminder for me to not judge a person by appearances. This young man was a somebody, not a nobody, with deep needs, not a hoodlum as many might assume. Experiences like this have helped me to see people the way God might see them. Their hearts often look quite different from their appearance.

Now this kind of thing happens nearly every time I leave the house and get around people. I usually get responses of hugs and tears of hope. Once I stopped at a garage sale, and the people running the sale asked about my head. I said, "Oh yah, I always forget I'm bald until people look at me funny or come right out and ask questions." And I shared my story again. I felt as if the Holy Spirit were talking through me to these wonderful people who seemed hungry to hear more about God.

The shortest time spent on my story was when a woman ran after me at a K-Mart, shouting, "Hey, hey, you. Stop!"

I nervously turned. "Me?"

"I have to see your head." Looking all around it, she exclaimed, "It's so beautiful and full of detail."

I thanked her and then saw she had a small teardrop tattooed under her left eye. "Did something sad happen to you?"

"Yes and no. This tear is to remind me that God will wipe away all my tears once I go home to heaven."

I pointed to my own head and said, "Flowers of Heaven." She embraced me and cried. That was all I needed to say. My shortest message to this day. That small tear was *her* message.

As for David, he finally came around. He sees the many people who stop and ask about my "tats," and I think he's secretly proud of me for having the nerve to do something this extreme.

He almost dreads going out with me now. Nearly every time I get stopped and questioned by curious people. Poor David! Sometimes we're in a hurry, but if they ask or if I sense God's prompting me to share the entire story, I do. A simple trip to the grocery store can take two hours.

Since the original inking, I've had the flowers' colors enhanced in four more sessions with another artist. She corrected the yellow flowers to be exactly as I saw them in heaven. This was important to me.

She also made the flower colors more vibrant and connected them with leaves and vines. Instead of individual flowers, they now look the way they did when they grew in Grandma's garden.

I get lots of stares when I go out. I get asked lots of questions. And I get lots of thumbs up and "You go, girl!" I'm surprised that I've received so little negative feedback.

I expected that at least older people would judge me harshly. But they haven't. They either tell me they love it, or they ask me why I did it. I occasionally get requests to speak at retirement homes, and their responses are always positive. They gain hope for their own future and encourage me to keep telling my story.

Children point and sometimes say, "Look, Mommy, at all the pretty flowers!" I gave my talk to a group of children who came from poor families and had few toys. Little hands shot up quicker than I could answer. They asked questions like, "Will I have a comfortable bed to sleep in when I get to heaven?" "Will I have plenty of good food to eat?" "Will I finally get an Xbox?"

Everybody's got a different agenda, but God always gives hope.

Chapter 12

YOUR TURN

Do not merely listen to the word, and so deceive yourselves.
Do what it says (James 1:22).

When something bad happens to you—and it will—you have a choice. You always have a choice.

You may face anything from an inconvenience to a catastrophe. We all process our experiences personally and differently from how others do. What's unpleasant to one could be tragic to another.

Think of a hardship you might face. How will you react? Will you dwell on the negative and stop there? Or will you look for a positive?

Somewhere in every negative thing that happens, a redeeming element is hiding.

Some may say, "What good thing could possibly come from what happened?" But look more deeply. You can find something good in every bad. It may be small, and it may be hard to recognize. But it's there, much like in diamond mining, a dirty and exhausting job. I've never seen diamonds growing on trees or conveniently sprouting out of the ground. Commercially useable diamonds form deep in the earth and are thrust upward in volcanic activity. To find them, miners must dig through tons of dirt and rock. Even diamonds that are washed away onto shorelines and riverbeds need to be dug and sifted.

Once you find that diamond in the dirt, a positive point in the midst of misery, what can you do about it? If I were you, I'd act on it. I've been told time after time that I always have a beaming smile. People who know all the adversities I've encountered don't understand this at first. This is where *choice* takes the stage. I choose to be happy. I decide to dig for the diamond in the dirt pile. I make every effort to find the positive in any negative situation.

Though I wish I always had a cheerful personality, I still find myself reverting back to the old "dad" side of me. Thankfully this is rare. Since my trip to heaven, I'm driven to uplift both others and myself. I make a conscious choice to find the good in every day, even when the good is hard to find. Yet I can still slip, like when I discovered a contemptible scratch on the car. Just like my father, I got angry. I immediately went and pointed my finger at David. He calmly heeded my summons to the garage and examined the damage. What would cause a mark like that? Who drove the car? And where? We found that it was *I*, not he, who was responsible for the contemptible scratch. I felt defeated for having let my old self creep back in. I couldn't apologize to David enough. He told me that in my imperfection I was becoming perfect because I realized my mistake and felt complete remorse. I acted on this by correcting my bad behavior. I'd like to be perfect now that I have been to heaven, but the fact is I'm still a human stuck on earth. As long as I'm here, I'll keep learning and growing.

And I choose to smile.

Your diamond could be less of a smile and more of a situation. One of the saddest times in my life was placing my mother in a nursing home where she would live out the rest of her life gradually succumbing to the clutches of Alzheimer's. Yet if that hadn't happened, I would never have become close to my father. I was *forced* to care for him when Mom couldn't. At first I resented this and wished he were dead. But over time I decided to put on a decent show and care for him anyway. My show turned to a reality in my heart, my father changed, and our relationship was healed. How terrible it would have been if he had died with me still wanting to dance on his grave. Instead we grew close and loved one another.

It is up to each person to choose whether to find that positive and then to act on it.

I'm convinced that every one of us has a story to tell. So what if yours isn't earthshaking? It's still real, and somebody will benefit by hearing it.

And if God is part of your life, that story takes on an eternal dimension, both for you and for others. The Bible has a promise to those who commit themselves in faith, saying that God "anointed us, set his seal of ownership on us, and put his Spirit in our hearts as a deposit, guaranteeing what is to come" (2 Corinthians 1:22). Metaphorically speaking, this is similar to being inked, *kind of like a tattoo on our hearts. Gasp!*

I am definitely not advocating getting tattoos, and please don't copy me. Think about your own uniqueness and your own spiritual or personal journey. How can you express it? How can you be an encouragement or a blessing to others?

Recently I talked with a woman who was feeling stagnant in her life. Everything was normal to the point of mindless comfort. She had no marital problems, her children were poster kids, and she'd never experienced a death in the family. Her spiritual life was okay, but she felt hollow and longed for a reason to have her own beaming smile. She craved a sense of purpose that could bring her fulfillment or at least happiness.

"My faith is strong," she said. "I have admitted my sins and have been forgiven, but something is missing."

I asked her, "Have you discovered your own story? If you have, are you telling it?"

"No." Then her face lit up. She realized she had homework to do—discern her story, find her voice, and use it.

If you're like her and think you don't have a story, I insist on telling you: You do. Without you something is missing in the lives of others. You probably won't get your head tattooed, but you still have a message to share. Maybe one you haven't thought about.

How have you suffered and survived, or struggled and overcome?

Has God done anything in your life?

Has another person sacrificially helped you?

Have you sacrificially helped someone else?

The things you've learned or achieved, the ways you've grown or been blessed—these define your message. And any feeling you have about them will motivate you and what you say.

What is *your* message?

I'm also convinced that every one of us has a purpose—a reason to be alive that leads us to live in a way that benefits others.

Your purpose may be big or small. You may do your thing in front of an audience or behind the scenes. You might get paid for it; you might not. It could be simple; it could be a complex combination of things. Even if few people know who you are, your purpose will still touch someone. And to that someone, you are important.

If you have a sense of why you're alive or what you ought to do with your life, you're standing on the path of fulfilling your purpose.

And if you grow toward being that person and do things that benefit others, you're walking that path.

How would you describe all that in your own life?

To whom are you important? Don't be shy.

And even if you sometimes feel worthless or lonely, think of yourself as a thread in the vast quilt we call life.

One thread would look awfully lonely on a quilt; it needs the intertwining of other threads. Each one—even the smallest—is important. And the big threads in fancy designs can't do it alone either. No one is so important that they don't need others. No matter which way you look at a quilt, if one thread is absent, the pattern is incomplete.

You cannot go through life without impacting other people, even in small ways. And the more we all realize this and act on it, the better we'll live out what we're made for. What part of a pattern will your thread weave?

As excited as I am to tell my story and fulfill my purpose, and as thankful as I am for each day, I always look beyond. I see that glimpse of heaven. The indescribable beauty, the overwhelming joy—I can't wait to go.

Our lives on earth are so temporary. And we can't take our money or our stuff with us. God has revealed to us what's important before we die and how to be in His heavenly presence after that. He loves us and has provided the way through Jesus' sacrifice for us on the Cross. Following Him is a small price compared to what He gives.

If you think about it too, I hope you wouldn't turn down the opportunity of such an eternity. Will I see you there?

Until then it's our choice to live well, no matter what. Because none of us knows how much time we have left.

Recently David and I found that he is also sick. He's been diagnosed with Amyloidosis, a rare blood disease that lives in his bone marrow. Like MS, this disease is unpredictable. And it is terminal.

We walked in silence from the hospital to the parking lot, letting the dreadful news sink in. The doctor hadn't said much. We had a short discussion about future chemotherapy treatments, but everything was "wait and see." David and I were in such shock that we never thought to ask how long he had to live.

We drove along a street lined with fast food and bargain advertisements. Life seemed normal for everyone but us.

I was supposed to die first, not him!

We began to discuss end-of-life care, and I determined to keep him home at all costs. Our sunroom would make the perfect hospital room for him. He could look out over our property and see the deer and other animals pass through our yard. I would make it a cheery place for him. But before it came to that, I wanted David to live the rest of his life doing the things he loves so much—fishing and hunting. I would support him all the way. I determined to never cry in front of him. He doesn't need that and would never know all the times I'd cried over this news.

I was reminded how short our lives are here on earth. The doctor's news caused me to cherish David even more. And cherish life more—as we look forward to heaven.

After driving down a highway for a while, David looked at me with worried eyes. "Well, now we're both sick. What are we going to do?"

I smiled back. "We're going to have the time of our lives."

EPILOGUE

By Peter Lundell

I have fallen in love with Roxanne and David. They have changed my life. The disease each of them carries could flare up and kill them within days. So they never know if they'll still be alive at the end of the week. Though they each face the shadow of death every day, they do not live in it. They choose to live in the light of God's presence because they know their afflictions are temporary and what is unseen is eternal.

To say a disease can kill, or to speak of death, is in the greater reality to speak of a transition. And in view of eternity, that transition is an upgrade. Because Roxanne was given a glimpse of heaven, she knows how much better it is than even the best we have on earth.

Knowing this couple is bittersweet. Bitter because I've come to feel what it's like for them to carry a malicious thief and killer in one's own body. Sweet because I've come to feel what it's like for life to change for the better because of it. They know the difference between what is truly important and what only seems to be.

Sweet because I've learned that nothing I might lose in life is worth more than gaining a mindset that lives in the meadow of eternity.

Sweet because I've witnessed how much they love each other, what that love costs, and that the cost only increases their love. David's love—and more than emotion, I mean how he's carried Roxanne through hellish afflictions for two decades—has inspired me to love my wife, Kim, more than I ever did before.

Sweet because they've given me a model to follow: Never let anything defeat me. I can stand up to *anything*, even if it's killing me, and determine not to let it destroy who I am. I will not merely endure; I will prevail, and rise to a higher level because of the affliction. In the process I expect miracles, whether they be healing or doing the impossible while afflicted because I've put myself in God's hands.

I often tell people that God loves us so much He lets us suffer. Perhaps after reading Roxanne's story you understand.

I pray you find ways to live out the story that God would write in your life.

CONCLUSION

The thought of writing a book had never even occurred to me. After I shared this story with my father-in-law, who encouraged me to write it down before I forgot the details, I was content to share it with churches, women's events, retirement centers, and people in grocery stores or on the street. That was my ministry—so I thought. God had other plans. Through a long chain of circumstances, He brought Peter Lundell into my path. Peter lives in California, and I live in Michigan. I had never met him or heard of him when we were introduced. Peter was already a successful writer of his own works but had never ghostwritten for someone else. God moved him into my life and into a new venture, which impacted him as well.

The idea of writing a book frightened me on many levels. Would it even sell? And the thought of sharing my life for the world to see almost stopped me several times. Would people still like me when I was finished? Would I embarrass my family? Would people say mean things to me or even hate me? I had become a changed person, but would others believe it? I am quite sensitive and doubted I could endure much criticism.

Reliving my childhood was so painful I almost gave up four times. I had pushed the pain deep inside, hoping to forget it, but Peter talked me through it all. Sometimes I became tired and distressed. Again Peter encouraged me. Many times I wrote through the night, afraid to sleep because I thought I would forget something. I slept with a note pad on my bedside stand for more than a year, waking up in the night with long-forgotten thoughts. I prayed fervently over what God would have me say. At times I felt as though my brain were a sponge being wrung dry. But Peter always managed to squeeze out one more drop.

In the end, God's purpose became clear. I was to write everything. People needed to know that their sins could be forgiven and cleansed. The consequences of our choices will be with us until the day we die, and I have many, but God does, and did, forgive me. I ask myself, "Why me?" Why would God choose someone like me, so stained up with sin, to receive the gift of heaven? I don't know. My body is becoming so wracked with the MS that I'm sometimes afraid I won't be able to carry out His purpose. Then God speaks back to those negative thoughts and tells me that in every situation He will sustain me to carry out His work.

My desire is to reach a million people with my story, but if I don't I would be content with only one. You are that one person. I have a passion to tell as many people as I can that God is *very* real and so is heaven, and knowing that will change your life. My experience in heaven was not a dream or a vision. It was tangible and touched my life and changed every aspect of it. That is the power of God. Please don't even take a chance of missing out on eternal life. I pray you will experience the fullness of God's love. I pray you will find that you too can overcome adversities. And I pray this book will give you divine inspiration.

ABOUT ROXANNE WERMUTH

Roxanne speaks all over the United States at churches, revival services, women's events, retirement centers, and multiple sclerosis groups. She also engages in print media, radio, television, and the simple-yet-important message of hope as she talks with people one-on-one every single time she leaves home. She gets stopped every time and asked about her tattooed head, which opens the door to talk about Jesus and heaven.

She focuses her message on:

- Making poor life choices and their negative consequences
- Facing impossible, life-altering adversities
- Severe depression and the desire to give up on life
- Losing everything to gain everything
- Her out-of-body experience
- Her glimpse of heaven
- Life after heaven
- The choice to overcome and find positives in any negative situation

To contact Roxanne Wermuth,
please visit www.RoxanneWermuth.com.